A **BIBLICAL**
POINT OF VIEW ON
SPIRITUAL
WARFARE

KERBY ANDERSON

D1564853

HARVEST HOUSE PUBLISHERS

EUGENE, OREGON

Cover by Dugan Design Group, Bloomington, Minnesota

Cover photo © Photodisc / Alamy

A BIBLICAL POINT OF VIEW ON SPIRITUAL WARFARE
Copyright © 2009 by Kerby Anderson
Published by Harvest House Publishers
Eugene, Oregon 97402
www.harvesthousepublishers.com

Library of Congress Cataloging-in-Publication Data
Anderson, J. Kerby.
A biblical point of view on spiritual warfare / Kerby Anderson.
  p. cm. — (A biblical point of view on)
Includes bibliographical references.
ISBN 978-0-7369-2527-3 (pbk.)
1. Spiritual warfare—Biblical teaching. I. Title.
BS680.S73A53 2009
235'.4—dc22

                                                                    2008032098

Printed in the United States of America

          09 10 11 12 13 14 15 16 17 / VP-SK / 10 9 8 7 6 5 4 3

Contents

SPIRITUAL WARFARE

SPIRITUAL WARFARE AFFECTS EVERYONE. In fact, the day you become a Christian, you are already involved in spiritual warfare. There is no place you can escape from this. There are no "safe zones" or "secure bunkers" where you can hide.

Sadly, many Christians do not even know there is a spiritual war taking place around them. They may even become a spiritual casualty and never understand what has happened to them. They may become mortally wounded in spiritual conflict, or become so emotionally spent or spiritually weakened that they are essentially no longer of any use to God.

Others may have less serious wounds from this spiritual conflict, but still be affected by the battle. They go about the Christian life but are not as effective as they could be because of the "battle scars" they carry with them.

Jesus never promised that the Christian life would be easy. In fact, He warned us of the opposite. He said in John 16:33 that "in this world you will have trouble (NIV)."

Anyone who takes even a brief look at the history of Christianity knows that is true. Jesus was beaten and crucified. Most of the disciples died martyrs' deaths. Millions of Christians have been persecuted through the ages.

Christians today suffer persecution in many lands, and all of us wake up to a spiritual battle every day. That is why we need to be prepared.

What is spiritual warfare?

The term *spiritual warfare* refers to the spiritual battles that take place in the unseen, supernatural dimension. Although these battles are unseen by humans, we can certainly feel their effects. And in the Bible, we are given specific instructions about this warfare.

First, we need to realize that the weapons we use in this warfare are not human weapons fought in the flesh. Instead, they are spiritual weapons such as truth and righteousness, with which we can tear down strongholds and philosophies that are in opposition to God.

> Though we walk in the flesh, we do not war according to the flesh, for the weapons of our warfare are not of the flesh, but divinely powerful for the destruction of fortresses. We are destroying speculations and every lofty thing raised up against the knowledge of God, and we are taking every thought captive to the obedience of Christ (2 Corinthians 10:3-5).

Second, the nature of this battle is different from that of an earthly battle. In Ephesians 6:12, Paul explained, "Our struggle is not against flesh and blood, but against the rulers, against the powers, against the world forces of this darkness, against the spiritual forces of wickedness in the heavenly places."

We can also have confidence because God "rescued us from

the domain of darkness, and transferred us to the kingdom of His beloved Son, in whom we have redemption, the forgiveness of sins" (Colossians 1:13).

Some Christians do not like the warfare imagery in the Bible, but that is how the spiritual life is described. We need to prepare for spiritual battle even if we would like to ignore the battle for truth and error as well as the battle for life and death that is taking place all around us.

Third, the Bible tells us that preparation for battle requires us to wear the right armor and have the right weapons, which include truth, righteousness, the gospel, faith, salvation, and prayer:

> Stand firm therefore, having girded your loins with truth, and having put on the breastplate of righteousness, and having shod your feet with the preparation of the gospel of peace; in addition to all, taking up the shield of faith, with which you will be able to extinguish all the flaming arrows of the evil one. And take the helmet of salvation, and the sword of the Spirit, which is the word of God. With all prayer and petition pray at all times in the Spirit (Ephesians 6:14-18).

The Bible also calls upon us to be strong in the Lord. We should be steadfast in our resistance to the devil. We can do this by putting on the whole armor of God and resisting Satan. Ephesians 6:10-11 says, "Finally, be strong in the Lord and in the strength of His might. Put on the full armor of God, so that you will be able to stand against the schemes of the devil."

Where does spiritual warfare take place?

Spiritual warfare takes place in various places in heaven and on earth. First, we should remember that God dwells above the heavens. Psalm 8:1 says that God has displayed His splendor above the heavens. Psalm 108:4-5 says God's lovingkindness is great above the heavens and that He is exalted above the heavens.

The Bible also talks about the battle in the heavens. When a passage in Scripture talks about heaven, it may refer to one of three places:

1. The first heaven is what we would call the atmosphere, where birds fly (Genesis 1:20, Psalm 104:12).

2. The second heaven is where the angels fly and do battle (Revelation 12:4-12; 14:6-7).

3. The third heaven is called "Paradise" and is described by Paul in 2 Corinthians 12:2-4:

   I know a man in Christ who fourteen years ago— whether in the body I do not know, or out of the body I do not know, God knows—such a man was caught up to the third heaven. And I know how such a man— whether in the body or apart from the body I do not know, God knows—was caught up into Paradise and heard inexpressible words, which a man is not permitted to speak.

Spiritual warfare also takes place below the heavens and on earth. This occurs on the face of the earth (Genesis 6:1; Acts 17:26), where Satan prowls like a roaring lion (1 Peter 5:8). And it will also take place in hell and the bottomless pit (Revelation 9:1-2; 20:1-3) and at the "lake of fire" (Revelation 19:20; 20:10-15), where final judgment will take place.

Should we describe such spiritual encounters as *warfare*?

Some Christians react negatively to using the term *warfare* to describe spiritual battle because it's a military term. They feel that the whole idea of weapons and warfare is not biblical. But the Bible speaks of the Christian life in terms of warfare. Paul declared that we are soldiers of Christ (2 Timothy 2:3-4) and said that we are to use the "weapons of our warfare" (2 Corinthians 10:4) in the course of spiritual battle. While it is true that we as Christians are to be peacemakers on earth (James 3:18), we are also called to do battle in the spiritual realm.

When we talk about war, our minds go immediately to the many wars the nations of this world have fought. And every one of those wars has its own unique characteristics. For example, the Revolutionary War was fought with muskets and cannons. World War II was fought with rifles, machine guns, tanks, and propeller airplanes. The Gulf War was fought with automatic weapons, jet planes, and smart bombs. Every war ever fought has its own unique set of weapons, strategies, and tactics.

Spiritual warfare is, by definition, different from military warfare, and thus has its own set of weapons and strategies. The enemy in spiritual warfare is Satan and those who have aligned themselves with him. Later in this book we will more closely examine the nature of this enemy; for now, we will focus on how we are to conduct ourselves in battle. We will look at our walk, our weapons, and our warfare by looking at Paul's instructions to the Christians in Corinth.

Our Walk

Paul wrote, "Though we walk in the flesh, we do not war according to the flesh" (2 Corinthians 10:3). Our war is not an earthly one but a spiritual one. So even though we walk in the flesh, our warfare is not fought in a fleshly manner.

For the battle to be successful, those who are threatened must be willing to stand up and fight. Many wars have been lost because good people refused to fight. And many Christians believe that the reason Satan has been so successful in the world is because either (1) Christians have been unwilling to fight, or (2) Christians have not even been aware of the spiritual battles going on around them.

To stand up and fight means we must we willing to separate ourselves from the influence of the world, and we must be willing to resist the evil that threatens our lives, our families, our communities, our nation, and our world.

Our Weapons

Paul declared, "The weapons of our warfare are not of the flesh, but divinely powerful for the destruction of fortresses" (2 Corinthians 10:4). One of the most important weapons of our warfare is the Word of God. Paul calls it the "sword of the Spirit" (Ephesians 6:17). We read in Psalm 119 that when the Word is in our heart, we will not sin against the Lord. The Word is a weapon that we can take to the outermost parts of the earth (Matthew 28:18-20).

We are also instructed to wear armor before we go into battle (Ephesians 6). We are to gird our loins with truth (verse 14). That means we need to define the truth, defend the truth, and spread the truth. We are also to wear the breastplate of righteousness (verse 14). That means we are to rely on the righteousness of Jesus and live holy lives. We are also to take up the shield of faith (verse 16). When we have bold faith, we are able to extinguish the flaming arrows of Satan. And we are to put on the helmet of salvation (verse 17). We need to be assured of our salvation and stand firm in that assurance.

Our Warfare

What is the goal of spiritual warfare? Paul wrote, "We are destroying speculations and every lofty thing raised up against the knowledge of God, and we are taking every thought captive to the obedience of Christ" (2 Corinthians 10:5). We cannot fight this war with physical weapons because our targets are not physical. They are intellectual and spiritual. So we cannot fight them with guns or planes or bombs.

The word "speculations" (which is sometimes translated "imaginations") refers to the mind. It includes our thoughts and reflections. So we should challenge the unbiblical speculations and false ideas of the world by countering them with God's truth.

We must fight this spiritual battle with our heart, soul, spirit, and mind. We have spiritual targets that must be fought with spiritual weapons. And our ultimate goal is to pull down the strongholds of Satan in this world.

Our Enemy

Who are we fighting in these spiritual battles? Scripture describes three battlegrounds for spiritual warfare—the world, the flesh, and the devil.

- When we fight spiritual battles in the *world*, we need to take God's Word into battle. Jesus admonishes us to go "into all the world and preach the gospel" (Mark 16:15).

- When we fight spiritual battles with the flesh, we need to resist Satan's temptations and conquer our sinful desires. Christians are called to lead a holy life.

- When we fight spiritual battles against Satan, we are told to resist him so that he will flee. We are to contend with him for the souls of men and women.

Ultimately our spiritual warfare is for the hearts, minds, and souls of the people whom we reach with the gospel. We are to preach the Word of God, defend the faith, and promote holy living among fellow Christians.

What are some of the weapons of spiritual warfare?

The weapons of our warfare are spiritual because the battle we are fighting is spiritual. Paul stated clearly in Ephesians 6:12, "Our struggle is not against flesh and blood, but against the rulers, against the powers, against the world forces of this darkness, against the spiritual forces of wickedness in the heavenly places."

We need to understand that ultimately we are fighting battles that take place in the invisible realm. Though these battles affect us in the physical world, they are taking place in the spiritual realm. This of course poses a problem for the Christian, for it is difficult enough to fight a battle with someone you can see. It is much more difficult to fight a battle with an invisible enemy that lives in the spiritual realm.

We should also realize that we are not warring against flesh and blood but against a spiritual enemy. So even though we might be tempted to think that people are our enemy, our *real* enemy is Satan and his demons. People are merely pawns in the heavenly chess game being played out in the world around us.

Earlier, we saw that to be successful in a spiritual battle we cannot use weapons of the flesh. Rather, we must use spiritual weapons. Paul wrote about this in 2 Corinthians 10:3-5:

> Though we walk in the flesh, we do not war according to the flesh, for the weapons of our warfare are not of the flesh, but divinely powerful for the destruction of fortresses. We are destroying speculations and every lofty thing raised up against the knowledge of God, and we

are taking every thought captive to the obedience of Christ.

Paul made it clear that we are not fighting against people (Ephesians 6:12), but rather against fortresses (2 Corinthians 10:4). The word "fortresses" (some translations use the word "strongholds") is a military term. It is used only once in the Bible. It describes a castle with walls, towers, and moats. A fortress is a place strongly defended by soldiers who plan to hold out for weeks or even months against any attack.

In the context of 2 Corinthians 10:3-5, "fortresses" are the false ideas that are found in places that promote evil and error, for Paul said we are to destroy "speculations...raised up against the knowledge of God." Those who are taken captive by wrong thoughts (Colossians 2:8) are to be released by the truth of the Bible so that they can take every thought captive to the obedience of Christ.

What are the weapons of the flesh? When we try to solve problems in the flesh, we often resort to arguments, coercion, or manipulation. Or we will form groups to carry out boycotts, pickets, and various forms of political pressure. But Paul said we are to use weapons that are "divinely powerful," which are much more effective for fighting spiritual battles.

What are those weapons? It is interesting to note that Paul did not list these weapons when he wrote to the church in Corinth. Therefore, we must assume the Corinthians were already aware of what those weapons are, based on other letters Paul wrote to other churches.

One obvious weapon is that of truth. Believers are given insight into both the earthly and heavenly realms because of what has been revealed in Scripture. We know what is behind the forces we wrestle with (Ephesians 6:12). Our problem is not people, but "principalities and powers." We are engaged in an invisible war with spiritual forces behind the scenes.

Another weapon is love. In fact, the Bible links truth with love ("speaking the truth in love"—Ephesians 4:15). Love is a very powerful weapon in spiritual warfare. We should not approach people in an angry or judgmental manner; we must speak the truth and do so with love (1 Corinthians 13).

A third weapon is faith. Faith is defined as "the assurance of things hoped for, the conviction of things not seen" (Hebrews 11:1). Notice that faith is a conviction of "things not seen." This is important because spiritual warfare is an invisible war. Faith is the recognition of this invisible world and the confidence that God is still in control of everything. Hebrews 11 catalogs for us the things that both godly and ordinary men and women did by faith. And we are to consider this great cloud of witnesses (Hebrews 12:1) when we act on faith in this world.

Another important weapon is prayer. We are told in 1 Thessalonians 5:17 to pray continually (some translations say to pray without ceasing). We are exhorted to pray about the circumstances we encounter and to use prayer as a weapon. When Paul spoke about Christians putting on armor to fight spiritual battles, he said that "with all prayer and petition" we are to "pray at all times in the Spirit" (Ephesians 6:18).

Yet another weapon is to serve others. Jesus said, "I say to you who hear, love your enemies, do good to those who hate you, bless those who curse you, pray for those who mistreat you" (Luke 6:27-28). When someone treats us wrongly, we are to do good back to that person. In doing so, we will stand out. Paul also gave specifics about serving others: "If your enemy is hungry, feed him, and if he is thirsty, give him a drink; for in so doing you will heap burning coals on his head" (Romans 12:20).

What are the different schools of thought concerning spiritual warfare?

Among evangelical Christians there are two major schools of thought about spiritual warfare. There are some (such as John Wimber and Peter Wagner) who talk about "power encounters" with demons. And there are others (such as Neil Anderson) who propose "truth encounters."

The truth encounter writers believe that power encounters are not necessary and instead take a more psychological approach to demonic power. They argue that Satan's hold on Christians will be defeated if we confront him verbally by using the following seven-step method:

1. Renounce involvement with false religions or occult practices
2. Choose to live by truth rather than deception
3. Choose forgiveness rather than bitterness
4. Choose to be submissive rather than rebellious
5. Live humbly instead of proudly
6. Choose freedom rather than bondage to sin
7. Renounce curses placed on your ancestors

They argue that when those steps are followed, the demons are obligated to release their victim from bondage. That is the essence of the truth encounter.

The problem with this perspective is that there is no example of a truth encounter in Scripture. Whenever Jesus cast out demons (or even in the few cases when the apostles cast out demons), it was *always* a power encounter. Never do we see Jesus telling someone to renounce occult activities or curses placed on their ancestors.

We don't see Him reasoning with demonized individuals or calling on them to believe the truth.

When a person is controlled by a demon, he or she has lost reasoning ability. He or she has lost the ability to choose truth over error, right over wrong. In Scripture Jesus confronted such demons and cast them out. This is a power encounter with the spiritual world.

Where should we get our information about spiritual warfare?

The answer, of course, is the Bible. Unfortunately, many Christian books about the spiritual world are full of anecdotes and stories about demons and spiritual warfare with only a smattering of biblical texts to support the conclusions stated in the book. Usually the conclusions are based upon demonic experiences and not Scripture.

Thomas Ice and Robert Dean make a distinction between someone who arrives at their conclusions based on empirical data and someone whose conclusions are based upon the Bible. They say, "The empiricist will gather all the information he can from those who claim to have had some experience with an angel or a demon, or those who have helped deliver people from demonic influence." The empiricist will collect these case studies and draw conclusions. "Even when the Bible is consulted with this process no matter how high the empiricist's view of Scripture, in practice the Bible is treated as just another voice or witness to demonic activity. This always results in adjusting the biblical teaching on demons until it fits with the conclusions of various experiences."[1]

Pick up a half dozen books on demons, spirits, or spiritual warfare and you will likely see this approach in action. Many of the books will be full of stories of experiences various people had in relation to spiritual warfare, including detailed descriptions of exorcisms. Occasionally you will find a Bible verse tucked in among the accounts. As a result, the teachings on demonic activity and spiritual warfare are based upon anecdotal statements and not careful biblical exegesis.

In every matter, the Bible should be our ultimate authority. Paul said that "all Scripture is inspired by God and profitable for teaching, for reproof, for correction, for training in righteousness" (2 Timothy 3:16). Peter wrote that "no prophecy of Scripture is a matter of one's own interpretation" (2 Peter 1:20), but rather, is due to "men moved by the Holy Spirit" (2 Peter 1:21).

The human writers of Scripture didn't interject their own ideas about spiritual warfare into Scripture. Rather, they recorded what God imparted to them. They were inspired (the Greek word for this is *theopneustos,* which means "God-breathed"). God revealed to them what was to be recorded in Scripture.

Not only is the Bible inspired; it is comprehensive. Peter said, "[God's] divine power has granted to us everything pertaining to life and godliness, through the true knowledge of Him who called us by His own glory and excellence" (2 Peter 1:3). The Bible is completely sufficient for instructing us in any spiritual matter, including spiritual warfare.

2

THE FLESH

IF WE WANT TO BE PREPARED to battle temptations and spiritual influences, we need to pay attention to the three areas from which we can expect spiritual warfare: the world, the flesh, and the devil. We also need to understand the differences between living in the flesh and living in the Spirit.

What three ways are we affected by spiritual warfare?

The World

When the New Testament uses the term "world," most of the time it is a translation of the Greek word *kosmos.* Sometimes this can refer to the planet earth (John 1:10; Acts 17:24). At other times it can refer to people who inhabit earth. In John 3:16 we read, "God so loved the world," which is obviously a reference to the people on earth. Or the term can refer to those who are estranged from God (John 14:17; 15:18).

But when we talk about the influence of the world on our spiritual life and our souls, we are talking about the worldly system in which we live. This world system involves cultural and philosophical beliefs and practices that are ultimately in opposition to

God. That doesn't mean everyone is evil or that the world's system is filled with nothing but error. But it does mean that the world can have a negative influence on our souls.

We are taught in Genesis 1 that after the work of creation, the world was good. But when Adam and Eve fell into sin, evil entered into the world and Satan took control of it. Adam and Eve's rejection of God's plan began a world system that has since been in opposition to God. This world system has spawned false religions, false philosophies, and a culture foreign to biblical principles. Each of these, in one way or another, has the potential to deceive us and thus take our heart away from God.

Paul warned us to not be conformed to this world (Romans 12:1). He also warned to not let our hearts and minds be taken captive to false ideas: "See to it that no one takes you captive through philosophy and empty deception, according to the tradition of men, according to the elementary principles of the world, rather than according to Christ" (Colossians 2:8).

The Bible teaches that many temptations come from the world system around us. We read in 1 John 2:15-16, "Do not love the world nor the things in the world. If anyone loves the world, the love of the Father is not in him. For all that is in the world, the lust of the flesh and the lust of the eyes and the boastful pride of life, is not from the Father, but is from the world."

The Flesh

We will devote the rest of the chapter to this, so for the moment let's begin by acknowledging that in Scripture, like the term "world," the word "flesh" can have different meanings. Sometimes it refers to our body—our flesh and bones (Luke 24:39; Acts 2:26).

In this context, however, flesh is a second area of temptation and thus an important instrument of sin. We see this in the fact that we are born with a sin nature (Romans 7:14-24; 8:5-9). The flesh is part of our bodies (Romans 7:25; 1 John 1:8-10) even after we have accepted Jesus Christ as our Savior. But the good news is that the flesh's power over us has been broken (Romans 6:1-14) so that we can have victory over sin (Romans 8:1-4).

The Devil

The ruler and mastermind behind the world system is Satan. Later we will learn more about Satan; for now, we will focus on the resources at his disposal to wage spiritual warfare.

As we have just seen, Satan can use the various distractions of the world system to draw us into sin, temptation, and worldliness. We read in 1 John 2:15 that "if anyone loves the world, the love of the Father is not in him." So the devil can use the world to turn our affections from God to the world.

Satan can also attack us through our flesh. He can entice our flesh with various temptations. First John 2:16 tells us that "all that is in the world, the lust of the flesh and the lust of the eyes and the boastful pride of life, is not from the Father, but is from the world." Satan can draw our attention away from God by manipulating the desires of the flesh.

Why should we pay attention to the flesh?

A major part of spiritual conflict in our lives is internal, not external. Our flesh is what causes us to resist God's direction in our lives and even rebel against His influence in our lives.

It is because of Adam and Eve's fall into sin that the flesh became corrupt and can have a negative influence upon us. God warned Cain that "sin is crouching at the door," and that "you must master it" (Genesis 4:7). Psalm 51:5 states that we come into the world as sinners: "Behold, I was brought forth in iniquity, and in sin my mother conceived me."

Paul wrote in Romans 3:9-10 that "both Jews and Greeks are all under sin; as it is written, 'There is none righteous, not even one.'" He also talked about the fact that we are born in bondage to sin (Romans 6:6-7). And he said in Ephesians 2:3 that we are all "by nature children of wrath." In other words, we are children of wrath because we are, by nature, born into the world as sinners. And as sinners we are deeply influenced by the flesh.

How does sin affect us?

God created the world and it was good (Genesis 1). He did not originally create Adam and Even as sinners. But when they disobeyed God (Genesis 3), sin came into the world. Ecclesiastes 7:29 says, "God made men upright, but they have sought out many devices."

Sin has had a profound impact on humanity. Job 15:14 describes the wickedness that is now part of the human condition: "What is man, that he should be pure, or he who is born of a woman, that he should be righteous?" Verse 16 goes on to say that humans are "detestable and corrupt" and that we drink iniquity "like water"!

Sin even affects children. Genesis 8:21 declares that "the intent of man's heart is evil from his youth." Proverbs 22:15 says, "Foolishness is bound up in the heart of a child." And Jeremiah 17:9 says that "the heart is more deceitful than all else and is desperately sick; who can understand it?"

What this means is that we are born in bondage to sin (Romans 6). So before we become Christians, we are helpless in spiritual warfare. Yet even after we become Christians, we will struggle against the flesh, which is still present in us. Paul talks about this war within our bodies:

> We know that the Law is spiritual, but I am of flesh,
> sold into bondage to sin. For what I am doing, I do not
> understand; for I am not practicing what I would like
> to do, but I am doing the very thing I hate. But if I do
> the very thing I do not want to do, I agree with the Law,
> confessing that the Law is good. So now, no longer am I
> the one doing it, but sin which dwells in me. For I know
> that nothing good dwells in me, that is, in my flesh; for
> the willing is present in me, but the doing of the good
> is not (Romans 7:14-18).

Paul makes two important points: First, Christians may desire
to do good, and there may be times when we are inclined to do
it. But second, because of the flesh, sometimes we act contrary
to our desire to do good and we rebel against God's commands.
As Paul puts it, "I do the very thing I do not want to do."

The temptation of the flesh seems to be the primary means
by which we are spiritually misled. For example, in the New
Testament we can find more than 50 references to the flesh as
the primary enemy of the Christian. By contrast, demons or evil
spirits are mentioned only ten times (and most of these references
relate to factual matters about demons).[2]

What does it mean to live in the flesh?

In Romans 8, Paul sets forth a contrast between the person
who is living in the flesh and the person who is living in the
Spirit. He begins (Romans 8:5-8) by talking about the mindset
of a person living in the flesh:

> Those who are according to the flesh set their minds
> on the things of the flesh, but those who are according
> to the Spirit, the things of the Spirit. For the mind set
> on the flesh is death, but the mind set on the Spirit

is life and peace, because the mind set on the flesh is
hostile toward God; for it does not subject itself to the
law of God, for it is not even able to do so, and those
who are in the flesh cannot please God.

Paul points out (in verse 5) that those who live according
to the flesh have set their minds on the things of the flesh. Put
another way, they have a one-track mind. Sometimes when I turn
on the radio in my car, it isn't on the right station. That's because
it isn't on the right frequency. I can wait all day for the radio to
broadcast on the correct frequency, but that won't happen until
I change the frequency. People who live in the flesh are focused
on one frequency: their flesh!

If a person is not saved, then he is not tuned into the spiritual
dimension. He is essentially on the wrong frequency. The correct frequency can be heard only when he is "tuned in" by the
Holy Spirit (1 Corinthians 2:6-16). And when Christians are not
living by the Spirit, then they may also be tuned to the wrong
frequency. By contrast, Christians who are living according to the
Spirit have their minds tuned to spiritual things and are open to
the things of God.

In Romans 8:6, Paul gave a second reason that those who
are in the flesh cannot please God. He said that "the mind set
on the flesh is death." Notice that Paul didn't say that it *leads* to
death. Elsewhere he said that, but not here. Rather, he said the
mind set on the flesh *is* death. This is consistent with what he
said about God's wrath being both present (Romans 1:18) and
future (Romans 2:5).

When Paul spoke of death in Romans 8:6, he didn't necessarily
mean physical death, although that can be true too. Here he was
talking about death as separation from God. A person focused on
the flesh is alienated from God. Those who set their mind on the

flesh are dead and thus alienated from God. Their "life" is limited to the physical world and their materialistic perception of it. Paul talks about this spiritual deadness in Ephesians 2:1-3:

> You were dead in your trespasses and sins, in which you formerly walked according to the course of this world, according to the prince of the power of the air, of the spirit that is now working in the sons of disobedience. Among them we too all formerly lived in the lusts of our flesh, indulging the desires of the flesh and of the mind, and were by nature children of wrath, even as the rest.

What a contrast—the "mind set on the flesh" is death. However, a person whose mind is set on the Spirit experiences life and peace.

In addition, a person living in the flesh is not only ignorant of God, but he is actively hostile toward God and God's law (verse 7). He hates God, rejects His authority, and resists His Word. The unsaved mind naturally rejects the things of God and everything He stands for. Consequently, an unbeliever is not going to follow God's commandments and live a righteous life. Thus, he "cannot please God" (Romans 8:8).

Paul then talked about how Christians are not to live in the flesh, but instead, in the Spirit:

> You are not in the flesh but in the Spirit, if indeed the Spirit of God dwells in you. But if anyone does not have the Spirit of Christ, he does not belong to Him. If Christ is in you, though the body is dead because of sin, yet the spirit is alive because of righteousness. But if the Spirit of Him who raised Jesus from the dead dwells in you, He who raised Christ Jesus from the dead will also give life to your mortal bodies through His Spirit who dwells in

you. So then, brethren, we are under obligation, not to the flesh, to live according to the flesh—for if you are living according to the flesh, you must die; but if by the Spirit you are putting to death the deeds of the body, you will live (Romans 8:9-13).

Notice that Paul instructed Christians to respond to the Holy Spirit that indwells them. This is done by faith, in obedience to God's Word, in order to deal with two problems: (1) the problem of sin, and (2) the problem of righteousness. Our problem with sin is that we do it. Paul said: "I do the very thing I do not want to do." Our problem with righteousness is that we want to be righteous, but cannot.

The solution to the first problem is salvation. God dealt with sin through His Son (Christ's death on the cross). When we receive Christ as Savior, our sins are washed away. The solution to the second problem is living in the Holy Spirit.

God's law sets the standard for righteousness. It is holy, righteous, and good. But we know that the flesh cannot please God. The flesh is dead because of sin. The Holy Spirit (who indwells every believer) is the same Spirit who raised the dead body of our Lord Jesus Christ (Romans 8:11). We can, through the ministry of the Holy Spirit, fulfill the demands of God's law and thus please God.

That is why earlier in Romans 8 Paul wrote, "There is now no condemnation for those who are in Christ Jesus" (verse 1). The righteousness that we could not achieve by ourselves (because of the death in our fleshly bodies) was accomplished by God through His Holy Spirit, who raises bodies to life.

How does the flesh influence us?

In Galatians 5:19-21 Paul provided a lengthy list of the works of the flesh and demonstrated what the flesh can do to our spiritual lives:

> Now the deeds of the flesh are evident, which are: immorality, impurity, sensuality, idolatry, sorcery, enmities, strife, jealousy, outbursts of anger, disputes, dissensions, factions, envying, drunkenness, carousing, and things like these, of which I forewarn you, just as I have forewarned you, that those who practice such things will not inherit the kingdom of God.

This list of 15 characteristics of the flesh shows how it can have a negative impact on our lives. The first group deals with sexual sin and sensuality; the second group relates to idolatry. The third group deals with problems that surface in personal relationships with other people. And the final group deals with drunkenness and carousing.

Let's look at each of these 15 characteristics in more detail:

1. *Immorality*—this is the Greek word *porneia,* which is the root word for the English word *pornography.* However, in the context of Galatians 5:19-21, it includes any sexual activity apart from God-ordained marriage.

2. *Impurity*—could include sexual sin, but would also include impure thoughts and actions. So this would focus especially on sexuality but would not be limited to sex itself.

3. *Sensuality*—this would include sensual living, such as when one's sexual appetite and other appetites are out of control. It could also include sexual jokes and innuendos.

4. *Idolatry*—while this would include the worship of idols, it can also refer to anything that becomes an idol in our lives (anything that we put ahead of Jesus Christ).

5. *Sorcery*—this is the Greek word *pharmakia,* from which we get the English word *pharmaceutical.* In the ancient world, sorcery involved the taking of hallucinogenic drugs. Today this would include taking drugs as well as participating in various forms of the occult.

6. *Enmities*—this is a hatred for others that manifests itself in anger, grudges, or a desire for retaliation. This word is found in Ephesians 2:15 to describe the enmity (or hostility) between Jews and Gentiles.

7. *Strife*—conveys the idea of quarreling. This often results when we serve our desires rather than the desires of God. We not only find strife in the world, but also in many church congregations.

8. *Jealousy*—is the Greek word *zelos* and conveys the idea of wanting something or someone that someone else has.

9. *Outbursts of anger*—speaks of a sudden flash of anger. This refers to people who easily lose their temper and are unable to control their anger.

10. *Disputes*—this would include disagreements and selfish conflicts with another. The word has come to mean "selfish ambition."

11. *Dissensions*—comes from the Greek word *dichostasia,* which means "standing apart." In Romans 16:17 and 1 Corinthians 3:3 this word is also translated

as "divisions." This would include divisions and conflicts within the body of Christ or out in the world.

12. *Factions*—is the Greek word *hairesis*. It could also be translated "heresies" and would include false doctrines and cultic and heretical teachings.

13. *Envying*—the tenth commandment speaks against envy.

14. *Drunkenness*—the use of alcohol or other drugs. Although the Bible does not prohibit the use of wine or alcohol, it does admonish us not to be drunk (Ephesians 5:18).

15. *Carousing*—pursuing pleasure through parties and other forms of entertainment usually associated with drugs and alcohol.

Paul ended this passage by warning us about the impact that the flesh will have in our lives. Notice he said that these actions and behaviors are due to the flesh and not due to the world or Satan and his demons. They are the result of the flesh within us.

How are we supposed to deal with the flesh?

Paul began his admonition about the flesh with this command: "Walk by the Spirit, and you will not carry out the desire of the flesh" (Galatians 5:16). The concept of walking by the Spirit involves a continuous focus on God and a desire to develop biblical qualities in our lives.

When we walk in the flesh we are focusing on the flesh and what it can do for us. We are not dependent upon the Spirit; rather, we are totally dependent upon ourselves. It is possible for us to pray in the flesh, witness in the flesh, and even preach a sermon in the flesh. But Paul commands us to do these things in the Spirit and not the flesh.

When we walk in the Spirit, we are walking by faith. We are meditating on God and His promises day and night. We are trusting in Him continuously. When we walk in the Spirit, we are maintaining an ongoing communion with God.

In everything we do we have a choice: We can either follow the impulses of the flesh, or we can follow the leading of the Holy Spirit. Paul reminded us of the choices before us and the potential for spiritual battle in Galatians 5:17: "The flesh sets its desire against the Spirit, and the Spirit against the flesh; for these are in opposition to one another, so that you may not do the things that you please."

No Christian escapes this conflict between the flesh and the Spirit. You don't get a free pass from such struggles when you become a Christian. You will always face outward pressure and inner turmoil because of the war between flesh and the Spirit. In Galatians 5:18 Paul said, "If you are led by the Spirit, you are not under the Law." Notice he said, "*If* you are led by the Spirit..." This implies that we must make a choice of either living in the flesh or being led by the Spirit. Romans 8:14 speaks of those "who are led by the Spirit," which again speaks of the choice before us.

To live by the flesh is to depend upon your own gifts, abilities, and resources. To live by the Spirit is to be dependent upon the resources of the Holy Spirit, whom God gives to us by grace through faith.

How can we know we are walking in the Spirit?

When we are walking in the Spirit, we will manifest certain attributes (or fruit) in our spiritual lives. Paul gives a list of the fruit that will appear in the life of a believer who is walking in the Spirit: "The fruit of the Spirit is love, joy, peace, patience, kindness, goodness, faithfulness, gentleness, self-control; against such things there is no law" (Galatians 5:22-23). Essentially this provides us with a checklist we can use to determine if we are walking in the Spirit or in the flesh.

Love

Through our relationship with Jesus Christ, we are able to show love to others. The Greek word Paul used here is *agape.* This speaks of a selfless love for others.

The New Testament gives us more perspective on what this kind of love looks like: "Love is patient, love is kind. It does not envy, it does not boast, it is not proud. It is not rude, it is not self-seeking, it is not easily angered, it keeps no record of wrongs. Love does not delight in evil but rejoices with the truth. It always protects, always trusts, always hopes, always perseveres. Love never fails" (1 Corinthians 13:4-8 NIV). We also read in 1 John 4:16 that "God is love. Whoever lives in love lives in God, and God in him" (NIV).

Joy

Joy is more than just happiness or a pleasant experience. It is the manifestation of an inner delight toward life even in the midst of difficult circumstances. In the Old Testament we read that "the joy of the LORD is [our] strength" (Nehemiah 8:10). In the New Testament the writer of Hebrews said, "Let us fix our eyes on Jesus, the author and perfecter of our faith, who for the joy set before him endured the cross, scorning its shame, and sat down at the right hand of the throne of God" (12:2 NIV).

Peace

Peace is the opposite of stress or anxiety in our lives. Paul said that because "we have been justified through faith, we have peace with God through our Lord Jesus Christ" (Romans 5:1 NIV). He later concluded, "May the God of hope fill you with all joy and peace as you trust in him, so that you may overflow with hope by the power of the Holy Spirit" (Romans 15:13 NIV). He also admonished, "Be anxious for nothing, but in everything by prayer and supplication with thanksgiving let your requests be made known to God. And the peace of God, which surpasses all comprehension, will guard your hearts and your minds in Christ Jesus" (Philippians 4:6-7).

Patience

The original Greek word used for "patience" is also translated "longsuffering." In other words, we may suffer for a time as we choose to not respond in kind to threats from others. If we depend upon the Lord, we will be "strengthened with all power, according to His glorious might, for the attaining of all steadfastness and patience" (Colossians 1:11). As believers we are to be characterized by "humility and gentleness, with patience, showing tolerance for one another in love" (Ephesians 4:2).

Kindness

This word is sometimes translated as gentleness. It is an attitude that we are to have as we interact with others. Elsewhere, Paul said that believers should live "in purity, understanding, patience and kindness; in the Holy Spirit and in sincere love; in truthful speech and in the power of God; with weapons of righteousness in the right hand and in the left" (2 Corinthians 6:6-7 NIV).

Goodness

Goodness describes our actions toward others. Elsewhere Paul spoke about the fruit of the Spirit in this way: "The fruit of the Spirit is in all goodness, righteousness, and truth" (Ephesians 5:9 NKJV). He also said, "We pray always for you, that our God would count you worthy of this calling, and fulfill all the good pleasure of His goodness and the work of faith with power" (2 Thessalonians 1:11 NKJV).

Faithfulness

Faithfulness is the idea of loyalty and dependability. This would include loyalty to God as well as to the church and our families. In the Old Testament we read this of God: "O LORD, thou art my God; I will exalt thee, I will praise thy name; for thou hast done wonderful things; thy counsels of old are faithfulness and truth" (Isaiah 25:1 KJV). Paul prayed for believers "that Christ may dwell in your hearts through faith" (Ephesians 3:17).

Gentleness

This word is also translated "meekness." This doesn't mean that we are to be weak or allow others to take advantage of us. Rather, it means we are to be humble servants. We are to deal with one another "with all lowliness and gentleness, with long-suffering, bearing with one another in love" (Ephesians 4:2 NKJV). It is also how we are to restore one another: "Brethren, if a man be overtaken in a fault, ye which are spiritual, restore such a one in the spirit of meekness; considering thyself, lest thou also be tempted" (Galatians 6:1 KJV).

Self-control

This can also be translated as temperance. This implies self-discipline and an ability to control one's emotions and appetites. Peter talks about the importance of self-control in living the

Christian life: "For this very reason, giving all diligence, add to your faith virtue, to virtue knowledge, to knowledge self-control, to self-control perseverance, to perseverance godliness, to godliness brotherly kindness, and to brotherly kindness love" (2 Peter 1:5-7 NKJV).

We are in a spiritual battle, and much of that battle involves struggles with the flesh. We should carefully evaluate our lives and make no provision for the flesh (Romans 13:14). If we focus on the flesh, we will naturally walk in the flesh. But if we learn to walk in the Spirit and walk by faith, we will have victory over sin and in our spiritual battles.

3

SPIRITUAL ARMOR

YOU CANNOT BE EFFECTIVE in warfare unless you wear protective gear. The same is true when it comes to spiritual warfare. In Ephesians 6, the apostle Paul spoke of the need for us to put on spiritual armor to fight spiritual battles. What is our spiritual armor? How do we put it on? And how can we avoid spiritual deception and defeat?

What is our spiritual armor?

How do we prepare for battle in the spiritual realm? Paul said we are to "put on the full armor of God" (Ephesians 6:11). This is how we can stand up to our spiritual adversary.

Paul began by admonishing us to "be strong in the Lord and in the strength of His might" (Ephesians 6:10). This means we need to recognize that ultimately, the battle is the Lord's. We need to depend on His strength and not our own.

Paul also pointed out who the enemy is: "Our struggle is not against flesh and blood, but against the rulers, against the powers, against the world forces of this darkness, against the spiritual forces of wickedness in the heavenly places" (Ephesians 6:12). Our enemy is Satan and his demons. He wants us to doubt our salvation and the Word of God. He will distract us with worldly things so that we won't focus on spiritual things.

Because our enemy is spiritual in nature, we cannot fight our battles with fleshly weapons (2 Corinthians 10:3-5). Instead, we are to "take up the full armor of God" (Ephesians 6:13). We can only be successful if we "dress for success" according to the instructions in Ephesians 6.

Paul was definitely familiar with the language of warfare. He was a Roman citizen and no doubt witnessed military activity during his travels. He also spent long periods of time in prison and saw the armor of the Roman soldiers who guarded him. When Paul talked about armor, weapons, and warfare, he was helping us to better understand the spiritual battles taking place around us.

Paul made it clear that this armor is the only way we can stand firm (Ephesians 6:11,13-14). Satan is powerful, but God has given us *His* power ("greater is He who is in you than he who is in the world"—1 John 4:4). Yet we must put on the armor of God because of the coming of the "evil day" (Ephesians 6:13).

In a sense, when we endeavor to stand firm as we fight spiritual battles, we are working to defend ground that Jesus has already won for us through His death and resurrection. And standing firm against the attacks of Satan is more than just resisting Satan; it involves standing firm in the faith (1 Corinthians 16:13).

The spiritual armor described in Ephesians 6 is divided into two categories. The first three items are those we already *have* (having girded, having put, having shod). The second three are those we are to *take up*. In other words, we *wear* the first three, and we are to *pick up* the second three on a daily basis.

Let's look at each of these six pieces of armor in detail:

Belt

"Stand firm therefore, having girded your loins with truth" (Ephesians 6:14). The Roman soldier wore a long tunic that reached all the way to his ankles. Before he could fight, he would have to gird up his tunic by taking the ends and tucking them into his belt.

The belt (or girdle) on a Roman soldier was made of leather and metal and was very important for helping to carry the sword. Also, the breastplate was attached to the belt. So the belt was an important element of the armor.

Likewise, truth is important in our dealing with spiritual warfare. Satan counterfeits truth, so we must be able to present the unvarnished truth and expose his lies. Truth wrapped in a lie is still a lie. A discerning Christian must be able to handle the word of truth (2 Timothy 2:15) and expose Satan's lies.

Breastplate

Another part of our armor is "the breastplate of righteousness" (Ephesians 6:14). For a Roman soldier, the breastplate was a protective vest that was made of leather and often overlaid with metal. It protected his upper body from flying arrows or strikes from a sword. Most importantly, the breastplate protected the soldier's heart from harm.

Our righteousness comes not from ourselves but from Christ's righteousness that was placed upon us. His righteousness in our lives protects us from the intrusion of Satan and his demons. Essentially, it protects our hearts.

Shoes

"Shod your feet with the preparation of the gospel of peace"

(Ephesians 6:15). We are to walk in the "gospel of peace." The gospel is good news, and it is a message we are to bring to the world.

Often a Roman soldier's shoes would have spikes or nails on the sole. These would help him to stand firm. Likewise, we as Christians are to stand firm (Ephesians 6:11,13-14).

Shield

We are to take up "the shield of faith with which you will be able to extinguish all the flaming arrows of the evil one" (Ephesians 6:16). A Roman soldier carried a shield into battle for protection. When a soldier stood shoulder to shoulder with his fellow soldiers, their shields would help form an almost impenetrable barrier.

The "shield of faith" that we are to take up daily protects us from any arrows Satan might launch at us. We cannot prevent Satan from firing those arrows, but the shield of faith can protect us from them.

Helmet

We are also told to take "the helmet of salvation" (Ephesians 6:17). The helmet of a Roman soldier, which was often decorated, protected his head from blows that might have killed him or rendered him unconscious. The helmet was strong enough to absorb the shock of the blows of battle and allowed the soldier to continue fighting.

Likewise, the helmet of salvation protects our head. It allows us to continue fighting the spiritual battle and be victorious. Though Satan and his demons may hit us squarely in the head, we can still be effective for winning in spiritual warfare.

Sword

We are also to take up "the sword of the Spirit, which is the word of God" (Ephesians 6:17). Every Roman soldier carried a sword into battle. It was a little less than a foot long and was used for up-close fighting against the enemy.

We are to use the Bible like a sword against our enemy. Jesus provided an example of how to do this when He used the Word of God against Satan during the time He was tempted in the wilderness (Matthew 4, Mark 1, Luke 4).

How do we put on our spiritual armor?

The apostle Paul commanded us to "take up the full armor of God" (Ephesians 6:13). How is this done? After all, this isn't a physical kind of armor, but spiritual. Thus dressing ourselves with the armor of God involves our minds and hearts. Just as we put on clothes in the morning, we can put on the armor of God.

Belt

When you put on the belt of truth, you are choosing to focus on the truth, live in the truth, walk in the truth, and testify to the truth.

Breastplate

When you put on the breastplate of righteousness, you are calling on the Lord to protect your thoughts, emotions, and actions with His righteousness. You are calling for Him to keep you from being led astray by your emotions and by the temptations of the flesh, the world, and the devil.

Shoes

When you put on the shoes that bring the gospel of peace, you can ask the Lord to make you a peacemaker in the world. Also, these shoes with spikes or nails will help you stand firmly on the foundation of Jesus Christ.

Shield

When you take up the shield of faith, thank God for the ability to shield yourself from the fiery arrows of the enemy. You can stand securely in your faith because of the shield of faith.

Helmet

As you visualize putting on the helmet of salvation, you can thank the Lord that it will protect your mind. You can ask Him to put His thoughts in your head and protect you from any thoughts Satan might send your way.

Sword

As you mentally wrap your hands around the sword of the Lord, ask God to help you use His Word wisely and effectively and to allow you to deflect the blows of Satan as well as pierce the hearts (Hebrews 4:12) of those whom you meet.

Those are some basic steps you can follow each day as you attempt to "take up the full armor of God" (Ephesians 6:13). This armor is crucial for knowing victory in your spiritual battles.

What is the role of prayer in spiritual warfare?

Paul concluded his admonition about the armor of God by focusing on the role of prayer in spiritual warfare:

> With all prayer and petition pray at all times in the Spirit, and with this in view, be on the alert with all perseverance and petition for all the saints, and pray on my behalf, that utterance may be given to me in the opening of my mouth, to make known with boldness the mystery of the gospel, for which I am an ambassador in chains; that in proclaiming it I may speak boldly, as I ought to speak (Ephesians 6:18-20).

We can see the significance of prayer in the first word of verse 18: "with." The word "with" connects this section about prayer with the earlier discussion of spiritual warfare and the armor of God.

In addition to putting on the full armor of God, we must also pick up the weapon of prayer. This weapon can mean the difference between victory and defeat. Let's look at what Paul tells us about prayer and spiritual warfare.

First, Paul wrote that we should enter the battle "with all prayer and petition" (Ephesians 6:18). This seems to indicate we can use different kinds of prayer depending on the situation. Some people have used the acronym ACTS (Adoration, Confession, Thanksgiving, Supplication) to help themselves remember the various types of prayer. For example, there are times when we can lift up prayers of adoration and praise as we worship the Lord. And there are times when confession is included in our prayers because of a sin we have committed. Then there are prayers of thanksgiving because we are grateful to the Lord. And there are prayers of supplication, in which we petition the Lord for some need in our lives. We can use any or all of these types of prayer to help us be victorious in spiritual warfare.

Second, Paul admonished us to "pray at all times" (Ephesians 6:18). Our prayers should be ongoing because there are spiritual battles taking place around us at all times.

In 1 Thessalonians 5:17 Paul wrote that we are to "pray continually" (NIV). Some translations say we are to "pray without ceasing" (NASB, NKJV). This may seem impossible to do because we cannot always be on our knees and bowed down in prayer. But Paul was talking about our heart attitude. For example, when Paul told us to "rejoice in the Lord always" (Philippians 4:4), he was saying we should have an attitude of rejoicing. When he said we are to give thanks in everything (Philippians 4:6), he was saying we should have an attitude of thankfulness. So also we should have an attitude of prayer as we go through life.

Praying continually means that the lines of communication between God and us are always open. We are to be in fellowship with Him and allow the Holy Spirit to pray through us to the Father (Romans 8:26).

In the early church, we see many examples of praying continually. Acts 1:14 tells us, "These all with one mind were continually devoting themselves to prayer, along with the women, and Mary the mother of Jesus, and with His brothers." In Acts 2:42 we read, "They were continually devoting themselves to the apostles' teaching and to fellowship, to the breaking of bread and to prayer."

The Christians in the early church developed an attitude of devotion to and communion with God. We should do the same as we turn our hearts toward Him. God should be our first thought, not our last resort. We should seek His counsel before we seek the counsel of others.

Third, Paul said we should "pray at all times in the Spirit" (Ephesians 6:18). If we want to tap into spiritual power, we need to pray in the Spirit and have prayer that is directed by the Holy Spirit. Romans 8:26-27 says,

> The Spirit also helps our weakness; for we do not know how to pray as we should, but the Spirit Himself intercedes for us with groanings too deep for words; and He who searches the hearts knows what the mind of the Spirit is, because He intercedes for the saints according to the will of God.

The Holy Spirit is the third person of the Trinity and, by definition, is in touch with the Father's will. This is so helpful in the Christian life because often we do not know what to pray for and how to pray for it. Fortunately the Holy Spirit can direct our prayers, especially during times of spiritual warfare.

When we are fully dependent upon the Holy Spirit, He can speak to our minds and reveal to us how we are to pray. He can also lead us in prayer and give us spiritual direction and insight.

Fourth, we are to pray with perseverance: "Be on the alert with all perseverance and petition" (Ephesians 6:18). Not only should we pray continuously, we should also pray persistently. We should be "on the alert" because the devil "prowls around like a roaring lion" (1 Peter 5:8).

Jesus taught a parable about a widow and a judge (Luke 18) to illustrate the need for believers to be persistent. And in Matthew 7:7 He said, "Ask, and it will be given to you; seek, and you will find; knock, and it will be opened to you." He called on us to ask, seek, and knock. Thus we are to be persistent in our prayer life.

Sometimes the answers to our prayers can be hindered by spiritual forces. Daniel eventually discovered that the answer to his prayer was delayed for weeks because of a demon who was the prince of the kingdom of Persia (Daniel 10:11-14). So persistence is vital.

Or, perhaps you are dealing with a besetting sin or addiction. You are being held in the bondage of sin and need God's power to escape. You can go to God in prayer and ask Him to help you. Philippians 4:13 says, "I can do all things through Him who strengthens me."

Finally, we are to pray "with all perseverance and petition for all the saints" (Ephesians 6:18). We are to pray not only for ourselves, but for others who are in the midst of a spiritual battle or may be suffering persecution. This is a command for what is called *intercessory prayer,* which is simply prayer lifted up on behalf of others.

Your prayers can have a profound impact on others not only in your community but around the world. Your prayers can bless others, encourage others, and uphold those who are in spiritual combat. You have a mighty weapon in prayer, and you should be willing to use prayer not only for your benefit, but the benefit of others.

What is spiritual deception?

Spiritual deception is the result of Satan's world system. People are inclined to believe a lie spread by Satan and his demons rather than the truth of God's Word. Not only are unbelievers subject to spiritual deception, but so are believers. They may choose to believe the deception rather than God's Word or they may be subtly seduced into believing the lie.

The Bible warns that in the last days, spiritual deception will take place on an even greater scale than ever before. There will be a departure from the true "faith which was once for all handed down to the saints" (Jude 3). Jesus declared that there will arise "false Christs and false prophets" who will "show great signs and wonders." They will be so convincing that they "shall deceive the very elect" (Matthew 24:24 KJV).

Paul also warned of deceivers and false brethren (Galatians 2:4) who will promote a false religion that will seduce believers into accepting false doctrine. Paul also wrote that there will be a time when believers "will not endure sound doctrine" and therefore will turn away from the truth of Scripture (2 Timothy 4:3-4). This should not surprise us, for Satan disguises himself as an "angel of light" and his ministers disguise themselves as "servants of righteousness" (2 Corinthians 11:14-15).

What does the Bible teach about spiritual deception?

The Bible says a number of things about spiritual deception. First, we are warned about how sin (and our sin nature) deceives us. Hebrews 3:13 warns believers not to be "hardened by the deceitfulness of sin." Sin keeps us from seeing the world clearly; it keeps us from seeing the world as God sees the world.

Scripture also alerts us to the possibility of self-deception. This can occur not only because of our sin, but also because we cannot see ourselves clearly. John spoke about how easily we can deceive ourselves: "If we say that we have no sin, we are deceiving ourselves and the truth is not in us. If we confess our sins, He is faithful and righteous to forgive us our sins and to cleanse us from all unrighteousness. If we say that we have not sinned, we make Him a liar and His word is not in us" (1 John 1:8-10).

James also admonished us not to be deceived (James 1:16). He then went on to say, "If anyone thinks himself to be religious, and yet does not bridle his tongue but deceives his own heart, this man's religion is worthless" (verse 26). And Paul said we should not be self-deceived but properly evaluate ourselves: "If anyone thinks he is something when he is nothing, he deceives himself" (Galatians 6:3).

Finally, the Bible warns us about false teachers and prophets who will try to deceive us. Paul warned, "There are many rebellious men, empty talkers and deceivers, especially those of the circumcision" (Titus 1:10). He also said these deceivers would be evil: "Evil men and impostors will proceed from bad to worse, deceiving and being deceived" (2 Timothy 3:13).

We should not be taken in by these deceitful people and their trickery: "We are no longer to be children, tossed here and there by waves and carried about by every wind of doctrine, by the trickery of men, by craftiness in deceitful scheming; but speaking the truth in love, we are to grow up in all aspects into Him who is the head, even Christ" (Ephesians 4:14-15). In another letter, Paul admonished, "Let no one in any way deceive you, for it will not come unless the apostasy comes first, and the man of lawlessness is revealed, the son of destruction" (2 Thessalonians 2:3).

The apostle John wrote of those who will try to deceive us: "These things I have written to you concerning those who are trying to deceive you" (1 John 2:26). He then went on to say that many such deceivers "have gone out into the world, those who do not acknowledge Jesus Christ as coming in the flesh. This is the deceiver and the antichrist" (2 John 7).

What are some common forms of spiritual deception?

In Matthew 7, Jesus warned about certain forms of spiritual deception. We should pay attention to the various ways in which we can be deceived by others and by those in the spiritual realm.

One form of deception comes through accepting the views and values of the majority without discerning whether they are right or wrong. In spiritual matters, majority rule is a dangerous idea. A majority of people can indeed be wrong, especially if they do not have spiritual discernment. For example, Jesus said, "Enter through the narrow gate; for the gate is wide and the way is broad that leads to destruction, and there are many who enter through it. For the gate is small and the way is narrow that leads to life, and there are few who find it" (Matthew 7:13-14).

People without spiritual discernment often arrive at conclusions without the help of rational thought and careful examination. They accept what the majority of people say, but this "herd mentality" is not biblical. For example, the majority opinion today is religious pluralism, which teaches that all faith communities and faith positions are equally true. In fact, one quick way to start a theological fight with non-Christians is to quote Jesus, who proclaimed the exclusive statement, "I am the way, and the truth, and the life; no one comes to the Father but through Me." Many people today say such a view is bigoted and narrow-minded.

A second form of deception is a naïve trust in anyone claiming to be a Christian and a spokesperson for God. Jesus warned that there would be false prophets and teachers who will deceive us. He said, "Beware of the false prophets, who come to you in sheep's clothing, but inwardly are ravenous wolves" (Matthew 7:15).

We should recognize that not all false teachers realize they are teaching false doctrine. A few verses later in Matthew 7, Jesus said that many of these false teachers are self-deceived (Matthew 7:21-22). They may call upon the Lord's name, and they may even perform miracles and appear to have power from God, but they are not speaking in Christ's name and they are even undermining the work of Jesus Christ.

A third form of deception results from not incorporating Christ's teaching in our lives. Jesus taught that we must not only hear His words but act upon them:

> Everyone who hears these words of Mine and acts on them, may be compared to a wise man who built his house on the rock. And the rain fell, and the floods came, and the winds blew and slammed against that house; and yet it did not fall, for it had been founded on the rock. Everyone who hears these words of Mine and does not act on them, will be like a foolish man who built his house on the sand. The rain fell, and the floods came, and the winds blew and slammed against that house; and it fell—and great was its fall (Matthew 7:24-27).

Just giving mental assent to the Bible's teachings is not enough. James reminds us that the demons believe the biblical teaching that God is one (James 2:19), but their knowledge of that truth does not save them. We must accept Jesus Christ into our lives and allow Him to bring true change into our lives.

How do we keep from being spiritually deceived?

The Bible provides some clear guidelines on how to keep from being spiritually deceived. First, we need to spend time in God's Word. The Bereans were known as those who "examined the Scriptures every day" (NIV) to see "whether those things were so" (Acts 17:11).

Second, we need to evaluate what we read, see, and hear in light of Scripture. Jesus asked of His Father, "Sanctify them through thy truth: thy word is truth" (John 17:17). We should love the Lord with all our heart, soul, strength, and mind (Luke 10:27), and we should use our minds to develop and apply a Christian worldview to every area of life.

Third, we should remain steadfast in the faith:

> All who desire to live godly in Christ Jesus will be perse-
> cuted. But evil men and impostors will proceed from bad
> to worse, deceiving and being deceived. You, however,
> continue in the things you have learned and become
> convinced of, knowing from whom you have learned
> them (2 Timothy 3:12-14).

And last, we need to oppose false teachers and their doc-trines. Paul admonished Timothy to "fight the good fight of faith" (1 Timothy 6:12). This includes tearing down strongholds and philosophies that are raised up against the knowledge of God (2 Corinthians 10:3-5).

4

SATAN

ALTHOUGH WE LIVE IN a society in which a majority of people believe in the existence of spiritual beings, they don't believe in Satan. They may attribute evil in the world to human behavior or even evil forces, but they don't believe there is a fallen angel named Satan.

By contrast, Jesus and His disciples spoke about Satan. Paul referred to Satan as an "angel of light" (2 Corinthians 11:14). As we will see, he was created like the rest of the angels. But Satan was prideful and fell, and he took other angels with him in a rebellion against God.

Does Satan really exist?

Some Christians think that belief in Satan is optional. After all, they argue, if a person believes in Jesus, that is enough. But anyone who believes that Jesus is God—and that God knows all things—would have to believe that Satan exists. Satan is mentioned in the Gospels 29 times, and 25 of those references are from Jesus.

Satan is mentioned many other times in the Bible—we read

of him in seven Old Testament books and in every New Testament book.

In the New Testament, Satan is identified by three titles. These titles describe his power on earth and his influence in the world:

Ruler of the World

Jesus referred to Satan as "the ruler of this world" (John 12:31; 16:11; see also 14:30). This means Satan can use the elements of society, culture, and government to achieve his evil ends in this world. It doesn't mean that every aspect of society or culture is evil, and it doesn't mean that Satan has complete control of every politician or governing authority. But it does mean that Satan can use and manipulate various aspects of the world system.

God of this World

Paul said that Satan is "the god of this world," and that he "has blinded the minds of the unbelieving so that they might not see the light of the gospel of the glory of Christ, who is the image of God" (2 Corinthians 4:4). Satan sets himself up as a false god to many. His power over religion and the ability to promote false religions keeps people from knowing the true gospel.

Prince of the Air

Paul wrote that we who are Christians were once dead in our trespasses and that we "formerly walked according to the course of this world, according to the prince of the power of the air." Satan is the prince of the air and thus controls the thoughts of those in the world system. The Bible says, "The whole world lies in the power of the evil one" (1 John 5:19). So we should not be surprised that we find ourselves in the midst of spiritual warfare.

How did Satan fall?

The Bible doesn't say much about Satan's fall. There are two passages in Scripture that many believe are descriptions of Satan's fall, but not all theologians are convinced. These passages are Ezekiel 28:11-19 and Isaiah 14:12-19.

In Ezekiel 28, the prophet Ezekiel predicted the coming judgment of the Gentile nations and referred to "the leader of Tyre" (verse 2), and later to "the king of Tyre" (verse 12). These do not seem to be the same person. The first is obviously the earthly leader of the city Tyre, and Ezekiel was predicting his ultimate downfall and the destruction of his kingdom.

The one referred to as "the king of Tyre" seems to be a different person. He has "the seal of perfection" (verse 12) and was "blameless" (verse 15). He is described as "full of wisdom and perfect in beauty" (verse 12). We also read that he was "in Eden, the garden of God" (verse 13).

There are other indications that this person may be Satan. He was an "anointed cherub who covers" (verse 14) and a "covering cherub" (verse 16). Earlier in the book, Ezekiel saw "four living beings" (Ezekiel 1:5) who are later described as cherubim (Ezekiel 10:5-9). These descriptions would apply to an angel and seem to indicate the types of responsibilities Satan had before he fell.

It appears that "the king of Tyre" describes Satan, who was serving God as an angel. The passage further says that Satan was "lifted up" because of his beauty, which many commentators suggest means he was prideful as perhaps the greatest of all of God's creations. But he sinned. This passage says, "You sinned," and "You corrupted your wisdom by reason of your splendor" (verses 16-17).

Ezekiel also stated that Satan was "filled with violence" (verse 16) and was "cast" down to the ground because "unrighteousness" was found in him (verse 15-16). We also read that in the past, he was "in Eden, the garden of God" (Ezekiel 28:13). This is where Satan tempted Adam and Eve.

The other passage that appears to talk about Satan's fall is Isaiah 14. Here Isaiah predicted that God would bring judgment against Babylon. The first part of chapter 14 (verses 1-11) is directed at the king of Babylon. And many theologians and commentators believe that the subject changes in verses 12-19 because this portion focuses on the "star of the morning" (verse 12).

The words "star of the morning" in verse 12 could just as easily be translated "the shining one." That certainly connects with what we have already noted about Paul referring to Satan as an "angel of light" (2 Corinthians 11:14). Isaiah 14 also mentions that the one in verses 12-19 has "fallen from heaven." Thus it appears Isaiah is not talking about the Babylonian king, but about Satan.

If this passage is indeed talking about Satan, then it tells us more about what led to his fall. Five times in this passage we see the phrase "I will." Satan is prideful and wants to achieve a position "above the stars of God" (Isaiah 14:13). He also sought to be "like the Most High" (Isaiah 14:14). And he wanted to "sit on the mount of assembly in the recesses of the north" (Isaiah 14:13). Each of these desires tells us about Satan's motivations to usurp God.

First, Satan wanted to be superior to creation: "I will raise my throne above the stars of God" (Isaiah 14:13). This applies not only to the literal stars in the heavens, but seems to apply to all of creation (angels, humans, etc.). He wanted to rule over all of creation.

Second, Satan wanted to be superior to the Creator. "I will ascend to heaven" (verse 13) and "I will make myself like the Most High" (verse 14). Even though he already had access to heaven and God (the Most High), he wanted more. He wanted to be like the Most High, which is a title given to God as the sole ruler of heaven and earth (Genesis 14:18-19).

Third, Satan wanted a superior place to rule all of creation. "I will sit on the mount of assembly in the recesses of the north" (Isaiah 14:13). It appears that the mountain of assembly is a reference to Jerusalem (which is sometimes called the mountain of God).

We also know that after Satan sinned, he had "fallen from heaven" and was "cut down to earth" (verse 12). This passage also teaches that Satan will be "thrust down to Sheol" (Isaiah 14:15) in the future (compare to Revelation 20:3-10).

What do we know about Satan's character?

The Bible tells us a great deal about Satan through the various names that are given to him. Let's begin by looking at the name *Satan*. In Hebrew, the name means "adversary." Satan is opposed to God and His plans, which includes God's plans for our lives. If we are to be successful in spiritual warfare, we must understand that Satan is our adversary. This characteristic of Satan is significant; the Old Testament uses this name for him 18 times, and it is used 34 times in the New Testament.

Another common name for Satan is the *devil*. This name, in New Testament Greek, is *diabolos*, and is derived from the verb meaning "to throw." The devil throws accusations and lies at us while he slanders and defames the name of God. This name occurs 36 times in the New Testament.

There is one passage in the New Testament that uses both of the above names for Satan. Peter warned, "Your adversary, the devil, prowls around like a roaring lion" (1 Peter 5:8). He is a formidable adversary that believing Christians should not take lightly.

Satan is also known as the *tempter*. When he appeared to Jesus in the wilderness, he was referred to as the tempter (Matthew 4:3). He tempts us to follow him and his evil ways rather than God's plans for our lives. Paul also called Satan "the tempter" (1 Thessalonians 3:5), affirming the fact Satan tempts people to sin.

A related name is *serpent*. Satan took the form of a serpent to tempt Adam and Eve in the Garden of Eden (Genesis 3). Paul wrote about Satan's tempting of Eve through subtle craftiness (2 Corinthians 11:3).

One name the Jewish Pharisees used to describe Satan was *Beelzebul*. The Pharisees used this name in response to Jesus' casting out of demons (Matthew 12:24; 9:34; 10:25). They did not believe Jesus' power over demons came from God; rather, they concluded that he was tapping into the power of Beelzebul. The name most likely came from Baal-Zebub, who was the god of the Philistine city of Ekron (2 Kings 1:2). Also, the name *Beel-Zebub* (see Mark 3:22) means "lord of the flies." Essentially the Pharisees were saying that the power Jesus demonstrated over demons was demonic and from the lord of the flies. Jesus responded that their view was illogical: Demons would not cast out demons and thus work against themselves (Matthew 12:25-26).

Satan is also called "the evil one" both by Jesus (John 17:15) and John (1 John 5:18-19). Satan can control the world system, but believers are given the power to resist his temptations and evil designs. Satan is the source of much of the evil in the world, and that is why believers must reckon with his impact and contend with spiritual warfare.

We also see Satan's power as revealed in the names that describe his dominion. He is called "the god of this world" in 2 Corinthians 4:4. He is also called "the ruler of the world" (John 14:30) and "the prince of the power of the air" (Ephesians 2:2). And he is known as "the ruler of the demons" in Matthew 12:24.

How much power does Satan have?

The Bible gives us many examples of the extent of Satan's power (and the power of his demons). For example, the book of Job allows us to see into the spiritual realm as Satan and God discuss the life of Job. God provided a hedge of protection around Job, but Satan asked that it be removed. God allowed Satan to have limited power over Job and family: "Behold, all that he has is in your power, only do not put forth your hand on him" (Job 1:12). Satan therefore "went out from the presence of the LORD and smote Job with sore boils from the sole of his foot to the crown of his head" (Job 2:7).

Later in this chapter we will talk about Satan's temptation of Jesus, but it is worth noting here that the devil was able to offer Jesus all power and glory (Luke 4:6). This implies that he has control of the world system and can bestow power on those who follow him.

We learn from many Bible passages that Satan can affect people's minds. Paul, for example, warns believers that "the god of this world" can blind the minds of unbelievers (2 Corinthians 4:4). Acts 5:3 makes it clear that Satan can influence people's thoughts with temptations. He can give us nightmares (Job 4:12-16) and even cause emotional trauma (1 Samuel 16:14).

Satan can also affect the physical world. For example, he can engineer accidents (Matthew 17:15). Paul wrote that Satan hindered him during his missionary journeys (1 Thessalonians 2:18). And Satan can bring others into our lives who will hinder us (Matthew 16:23). And it appears from Hebrews 2:14 that Satan also has "the power of death."

How are we caught in the snares of Satan?

In some biblical passages (for example, Psalm 124), we read about fowlers and the use of snares. These hunters would capture birds by spreading a net on the ground that was attached to a trap or snare. When the birds landed to eat the seeds spread near the trap, the trap would spring and throw the net over the birds.

A snare can be anything Satan uses to entangle us or impede our progress. It can be a roadblock or a diversion. A wise and discerning Christian should be alert for snares, which can diminish our effectiveness and even ruin our testimony.

Before we look at the specific snares Satan uses, we should first do an analysis of Satan's strengths and our weaknesses. Knowing his methods and our vulnerabilities will help us to more effectively fend off his attacks.

We have already looked at the character of Satan, which has given us some insight into his methods and techniques. For example, Satan is referred to as "the tempter" (1 Thessalonians 3:5)—he tempts and entices us to sin.

James tells us that when we are tempted, we should not blame God. Instead, we should understand the nature of temptation and enticement: "Each one is tempted when he is carried away and enticed by his own lust. Then when lust has conceived, it gives birth to sin; and when sin is accomplished, it brings forth death" (James 1:14-15).

James shows that temptation toward sin is usually a process rather than a single act. We are tempted and then carried away and enticed by our own lust. Like a fisherman who tries to catch a fish using bait, Satan tries to entice us by placing before us something that will lure us toward sin. Then when the lust has conceived, we sin, and eventually experience death (spiritual death, perhaps even physical death).

James warned us that even when we feel like we are being spiritual, we may not be making wise, godly decisions. "You lust and do not have; so you commit murder. You are envious and cannot obtain; so you fight and quarrel. You do not have because you do not ask. You ask and do not receive, because you ask with wrong motives, so that you may spend it on your pleasures" (James 4:2-3). How many times have we wanted something only to later realize that we had not even prayed about it?

One way Satan attempts to snare us is through his lies. Jesus said concerning Satan, "Whenever he speaks a lie, he speaks from his own nature, for he is a liar and the father of lies" (John 8:44). Even when we sow the truth of the gospel, Satan spreads a lie. In the parable of the sower Jesus said, "Those beside the road are those who have heard; then the devil comes and takes away the word from their heart, so that they will not believe and be saved" (Luke 8:12). And Paul prayed that Christians would "no longer be children, tossed to and fro and carried about by every wind of doctrine, by the trickery of men, in cunning craftiness of deceitful plotting" (Ephesians 4:14 NKJV).

How then should we protect ourselves from Satan's snares? First, we should know our strengths and weaknesses. All of us have a sin nature (Romans 3:23), but we vary in the types of temptations we struggle against. But no matter what our weakness, God will not allow us to be tempted beyond our strength or ability to handle: "No temptation has overtaken you but such as is common to man; and God is faithful, who will not allow you to be tempted beyond what you are able, but with the temptation will provide the way of escape also, so that you will be able to endure it" (1 Corinthians 10:13). Remaining sensitive to the danger of sin, however, means making sure that we have not become "hardened by the deceitfulness of sin" (Hebrews 3:13).

Second, we should be prepared for spiritual warfare. Peter challenges us to "be sober, be vigilant; because your adversary the devil walks about like a roaring lion, seeking whom he may devour. Resist him, steadfast in the faith" (1 Peter 5:8-9 NKJV). Satan never rests; he is always on the prowl. For this reason we must always be on our guard and make sure "that Satan will not tempt [us]" (1 Corinthians 7:5). James also tells us to "resist the devil and he will flee. Draw near to God and He will draw near to you" (James 4:7-8). We should also "put on the full armor of God, so that [we] will be able to stand firm against the schemes of the devil" (Ephesians 6:11). A key part of standing firm is to wield "the sword of the Spirit, which is the word of God" (Ephesians 6:17).

Finally, we should also appropriate God's provision for us in our spiritual warfare. That is, we should be "filled with the Spirit" (Ephesians 5:18) and we should "walk by the Spirit" (Galatians 5:16). The Bible teaches that we have all we need for life and godliness (2 Peter 1:3). That's why it is essential that we depend upon the Lord's provision as we engage in spiritual warfare.

What are the snares of Satan?

Satan may not always be present in a given temptation. He will use circumstances and human agents to accomplish his purposes. But ultimately he will be the one at work behind the scenes. As the saying goes, "Behind the lie is the liar; behind the trap is the trapper."

Erwin Lutzer, in his book *Seven Snares of the Enemy,* acknowledges there are more than seven snares that Satan uses.[3] His book only begins to describe some of the most common snares and recognize that there are many others.

1. Greed

Greed is a key snare and illustrates what is in the heart. In the movie *Wall Street,* Michael Douglas plays Gordon Gekko, who lauds the value of greed. He says, "The point is, ladies and gentlemen, that greed, for lack of a better word, is good. Greed is right. Greed works."

Erwin Lutzer says that greed has two cousins:[4] covetousness (Exodus 20:17) and envy (Proverbs 3:31; Galatians 5:21). In order to avoid this snare, we must be willing to admit that these feelings exist in our heart and learn to be content in whatever circumstance we find ourselves (Philippians 4:11).

2. Gambling

Gambling affects not only the compulsive gambler, but those around him or her. In a sense, this snare arises from some other snares (greed, covetousness). It also surfaces because we are dissatisfied with God's provision for us.

3. Alcoholism

Alcoholism is a major source of family disruption and economic devastation, as is addiction to drugs. The alcoholic must realize that something else is controlling him or her. The Bible teaches that we should not "get drunk with wine...but be filled with the Spirit" (Ephesians 5:18).

4. Pornography

Pornography not only can control our lives, it also defiles our spirit. The Bible admonishes us to abstain from sinful desires (1 Peter 2:11) that war against our soul. Instead, we should live exemplary lives before the watching world (1 Peter 2:12).

5. Sexual Affairs

We live in a world of sexual freedom and we hear false messages from the media and our culture convincing us that happiness is just around the corner with the next sexual partner we meet. This is the myth of greener grass on the other side of the fence. But marriage should be "held in honor among all" (Hebrews 13:4).

We are not to unite our bodies with another in sexual immorality (1 Corinthians 6:15-16).

6. The Search for Pleasure

The philosophy of hedonism dominates our culture today. Erwin Lutzer says that perhaps the greatest of the snares "is the futile hope that our raging thirst for fulfillment can be met by the pleasures of this world."[5] We live in a society full of lovers of pleasure rather than lovers of God (2 Timothy 3:1-5).

7. Occultism

Movies and television shows promote the occult and make the dark side of evil look enticing. The Bible, however, warns us to avoid the occult (Deuteronomy 18:9-14). Anyone involved in the occult must repent of his or her activity and remove, from his or her life, any entry point (books, videos, games, etc.) into the occult.

How did Jesus resist the temptations of Satan?

We can learn some valuable lessons about spiritual warfare by watching how Jesus resisted the temptations of Satan (Matthew 4; Mark 1; Luke 4). The Bible records three attempts by Satan to get Jesus to act independently of His Father's will for Him.

Challenged God's Provision

Satan first challenged Jesus to turn stones into bread (Matthew 4:3). The Bible tells us that Jesus was very hungry after fasting for 40 days. While Jesus had the power to do this miracle, He resisted because it was His Father's will that He fast in the wilderness for 40 days and nights.

In response, Jesus quoted a portion of Deuteronomy 8:3 back

to Satan: "It is written, 'Man shall not live on bread alone, but on every word that proceeds out of the mouth of God'" (Matthew 4:4).

Challenged God's Protection

Satan next took Jesus into "the holy city and had Him stand on the pinnacle of the temple" (Matthew 4:5). He then commanded Jesus to throw Himself down so that God would send angels to protect Him. Satan wanted Jesus to take His protection into His own hands and no longer trust in God's protection. Notice that Satan even quoted Scripture (Psalm 91) to Jesus (Matthew 4:6) in order to tempt Him.

Jesus, in response, quoted a portion of Deuteronomy 6:16 back to Satan: "It is written, 'You shall not put the Lord your God to the test'" (Matthew 4:7).

Challenged God's Dominion

Satan then took Jesus "to a very high mountain and showed Him all the kingdoms of the world and their glory" (Matthew 4:8). Satan said, "All these things I will give You, if You fall down and worship me" (verse 9). Satan would give Jesus rule and dominion over all that the world could provide if only Jesus would turn away from His mission to save mankind and worship Satan.

Notice that Jesus did not challenge Satan's claim that he had the kingdoms of the world to give to Him. After all, Satan is "the ruler of this world" (John 12:31). But Jesus answered, "Go Satan! For it is written, 'You shall worship the Lord your God and serve Him only'" (Matthew 4:10).

When we engage in spiritual warfare, we can experience to a lesser degree each of the temptations that Satan placed in front of Jesus. Satan tries to get us to commit sin by acting independently of God. He will challenge God's provision, protection, and dominion in our lives. In every instance, Jesus responded with the truths of Scripture—even when Satan misused Scripture. And we too can look to the Bible as our "sword" (Ephesians 6:17).

We who are Christians can take comfort in the fact that Jesus understands the trials and temptations we face. "We do not have a high priest who cannot sympathize with our weaknesses, but One who has been tempted in all things as we are, yet without sin. Therefore let us draw near with confidence to the throne of grace, so that we may receive mercy and find grace to help in time of need" (Hebrews 4:15-16).

When it comes to Satan, we need to remember that he is a defeated foe. Jesus said that "the ruler of this world has been judged" (John 16:11). But his influence is still felt. John said that "the whole world lies in the power of the evil one" (1 John 5:19). And Peter reminds us that "the devil walks about like a roaring lion, seeking someone to devour" (1 Peter 5:8). The good news is that "greater is He who is in you than he who is in the world" (1 John 4:4).

5

DEMONS

ALTHOUGH MANY PEOPLE TODAY reject the idea of a literal Satan, more than two-thirds of Americans believe that angels and demons are active in the world.[6] As mentioned in the last chapter, most people attribute the evil in this world to human choices and spiritual forces. Even then, however, as Western society advances technologically, the idea that spiritual entities can influence our attitudes and behavior seems to become less and less prevalent. But when you travel to other countries, you will find that nearly every religious culture has some teaching about "spirit guides" or "evil spirits." And they have shamans, witch doctors, and healers to deal with these spiritual influences.

Do demons really exist?

Of course, these cultures and religions could all be mistaken. And that is the position most modern skeptics take today. They believe that people in other places have long attributed various medical and emotional problems to demons because they did not know there were physiological and psychological explanations for those problems.

But according to the Bible, demons really do exist. We find

both Old and New Testament examples of demons. Even more significantly, the Gospels contain numerous references to Jesus casting out demons. He didn't attribute these people's physical or emotional distress to physiological or psychological problems. He attributed them to demons, and He cast them out.

Where do we find demons in the Old Testament?

There are fewer references to demons in the Old Testament than in the New, but that does not mean they were not active during that time. Satan was certainly alive and at work, and we can see evidence of his demonic influence in the nations surrounding Israel, which were engaged in animistic and polytheistic worship. The people in these nations cast spells, used various incantations, and even carried out human sacrifice. Sometimes even the Israelites participated in these pagan celebrations. Deuteronomy 32:17 mentions those who "sacrificed to demons who were not God, to gods whom they have not known." And Psalm 106:37 refers to those who "sacrificed their sons and their daughters to the demons."

It is worth noting that even though these (and other passages) may use the word "demons" in connection with idol worship, the people of these animistic and polytheistic cultures viewed themselves as worshipping pagan gods, not demons. The Bible teaches that "the god of this world," who is Satan, blinds "the minds of the unbelieving" (2 Corinthians 4:4).

Are the "sons of God" in Genesis 6 actually demons?

Whenever I teach about angels or demons, I can be assured that there will be a question about Genesis 6:2, which talks about the "sons of God" who saw the "daughters of men" and took them as wives. Who were these "sons of God," and is it possible that they were demons who tried to interbreed with humans?

Some have argued that the "sons of God" were men who descended from Seth (considered in the Old Testament to be a godly line) and that the "daughters of men" were women from Cain (considered to be an ungodly line). The problem with this view is that the "daughters of men" are not limited to the descendants of Cain, and there are places in the Bible where "sons of God" obviously refers to angelic beings (for example, Job 1:6; 2:1; 38:7) rather than to men.

Another view is that the phrase "sons of God" refers to demons. These demons took the "daughters of men" and produced children known as Nephilim (Genesis 6:4). Ultimately, God judged the Earth with a worldwide flood and wiped out everyone except Noah and his family.

In the New Testament, Peter referred to demons who were cast into hell to be "reserved for judgment" (2 Peter 2:4). Jude 6 calls demons "angels who did not keep their own domain." These New Testament references seem to imply that demons might have been able to inhabit the bodies of men and thus produce the kind of evil offspring described in Genesis 6.

Some have argued against this interpretation because they believe that spiritual beings cannot have sex with humans. After all, Jesus said in Matthew 22:30 that angels are not given in marriage. But this statement only describes angels in heaven and not demonic activity on Earth. In fact, the emphasis in Matthew 22:30 is really on the fact that *humans* do not marry in heaven.

The Bible does teach that demons are able to roam the Earth and affect humans (Ephesians 6:12; 2 Peter 2:4; Jude 6-7). It is instructive that 2 Peter 2 seems to tie demonic activity to the flood of Noah.

Still another objection to the second view is this: Why would the Bible refer to demons as "sons of God"? If they were fallen angels doing wicked things on Earth, why would they be called "sons of God"? Perhaps the designation is simply to point out that God created them, even though it's true that they have set themselves up in opposition to Him.

Though Genesis 6:2 is a controversial passage, we need to remember that understanding its meaning is not a crucial aspect of living the Christian life. Godly men and women may come to different conclusions about the passage, which does not touch upon any of the fundamental doctrines of the Christian faith.

What about demons in the New Testament?

Most of the information we have about demons in the New Testament comes from the dealings Jesus had with them. His encounters with demons are linked to His claims to be the Messiah and their attempts to derail His message and mission. Beyond that are a few examples of demon possession that occurred in the course of the apostles' ministry, and Jesus had given the apostles power over "unclean spirits" (Matthew 10:1).

In the Gospels

The Gospels present four general statements about Jesus healing people afflicted by demons or diseases:

1. After healing Peter's mother-in-law, Jesus cast out demons in the townspeople (Matthew 8:16-17; Mark 1:32-34; Luke 4:40-41).

2. Jesus healed people of various diseases and demons in Judea and Jerusalem and the coastal region of Tyre and Sidon (Matthew 4:24; Mark 3:11; Luke 6:18).

3. Jesus cured many people of diseases and afflictions and evil spirits (Luke 7:21).

4. Jesus appears to have taught that some demons are more wicked than others (Matthew 12:45).

In the Synoptic Gospels

There are some specific incidents described in detail in the synoptic Gospels:

1. Jesus healed a demon-possessed man who was blind and mute (Matthew 12:22; Luke 11:14), and some accused him of casting out demons by Beelzebul, the ruler of demons.

2. Jesus commanded evil spirits to leave in a man in a synagogue (Mark 1:23-28; Luke 4:33-37).

3. Jesus cast out demons from two men in the Gadarenes and sent the demons into a herd of swine (Matthew 8:28-32; Mark 5:2-13; Luke 8:27-33).

4. Jesus healed the demon-possessed daughter of a Syrophoenician woman (Matthew 15:22-28; Mark 7:25-30).

5. Jesus cast a demon out of a man's son—the disciples had been unable to cast out the demon (Matthew 17:14-18; Mark 9:17-27; Luke 9:38-42).

6. Jesus cast out seven demons from Mary Magdalene (Luke 8:2).

7. On the Sabbath, Jesus healed a woman who had a sickness for 18 years—the sickness was "caused by a spirit" (Luke 13:10-13).

We also read that Jesus gave the 12 disciples authority over unclean spirits (Matthew 10:1; Mark 6:7). The Bible records for us that they were able to cast out many demons (Mark 6:13).

In the Book of Acts

In the book of Acts we find two mentions of the apostles casting out demons:

1. The apostles healed people brought from "the cities in the vicinity of Jerusalem." These people were "sick or afflicted with unclean spirits" (Acts 5:16).

2. Paul commanded a spirit to come out of a slave girl who was a fortune-teller (Acts 16:18). When this took place, the owners of the slave girl "saw that their hope of profit was gone" (Acts 16:19).

Do demons have personalities?

A common fallacy is to think of demons as evil robots without minds or personalities. Demons, however, are fallen angels who use their powers to fulfill the wishes of Satan. They can use their personalities to deceive believers and nonbelievers alike. In the next chapter, we will talk about the impact demons can have on a person who is being oppressed or even possessed by demons.

We see evidence of demon personalities in a number of biblical passages. First, Jesus conversed with demons on a few occasions and interacted with their personalities. For example, in Mark 9:25 Jesus said, "You deaf and mute spirit, I command you, come out of him and do not enter him again."

In Matthew 8, Jesus came upon two men who were demon-possessed. The demons cried out to him, "What business do we have with each other, Son of God? Have You come here to torment us before the time?" (Matthew 8:29). Then they said, "If you are going to cast us out, send us into the herd of swine" (Matthew 8:31).

The demons demonstrated personality in this exchange, and

Jesus dealt with them as beings that have personality. He addressed them directly, rebuked them and their influence, and then cast them out. He addressed entities with personality, not an inanimate force or power.

Second, demons show emotion (which is another aspect of personality). James wrote that demons fear and even shudder (James 2:19).

And third, demons have a worldview. Paul told Timothy about the demons' belief system: "The Spirit explicitly says that in later times some will fall away from the faith, paying attention to deceitful spirits and doctrines of demons" (1 Timothy 4:1). Evidently, demons promote a doctrine (no doubt a false doctrine) when they are in contact with human beings.

How do demons influence us?

In 1 Timothy 4:1, Paul talks about "deceitful spirits and doctrines of demons." In the verses that follow, we read of false teachers who attempt to convince believers that there are certain things they should avoid (such as specific foods and marriage). So one tactic of Satan and his demons is to tell us that things which God said are good are actually bad for us.

Another tactic that Satan and his demons use is just the opposite: that we should pursue things that God tells us to avoid. This happened when Satan tempted Eve in the Garden of Eden (Genesis 3). He tempted Eve to eat from a tree that God had forbidden her and Adam to eat from.

Demons also try to turn believers and nonbelievers away from the simple message of the gospel. Satan may not have been able to tempt Jesus to turn away from His message, but he can try to turn us away from that message. Paul wrote, "I am afraid that, as the serpent deceived Eve by his craftiness, your minds will be led astray from the simplicity and purity of devotion to Christ" (2 Corinthians 11:3).

In fact, Satan and his demons will even blind people to the gospel. "If our gospel is veiled, it is veiled to those who are perishing, in whose case the god of this world has blinded the minds of the unbelieving so that they might not see the light of the gospel" (2 Corinthians 4:3-4).

Satan and his demons use deception to lead many astray. This is done through "false apostles, deceitful workers, disguising themselves as apostles of Christ. No wonder, for even Satan disguises himself as an angel of light. Therefore it is not surprising if his servants also disguise themselves as servants of righteousness" (2 Corinthians 11:13-15).

What do demons know?

Only God is all-knowing (omniscient); Satan and his demons are not. But that does not mean they are ignorant. We learn from Scripture that demons have exceptional intelligence. Here is a short list of some of the things they know:

- We can see in Mark 1:34 that demons knew who Jesus was. When Jesus confronted them, there was instant recognition. In fact, the demons even called him "the Son of God" (Mark 3:11) and "the Son of the Most High God" (Mark 5:7).

- As mentioned earlier, demons can disguise themselves as servants of righteousness (2 Corinthians 11:15). To do this they must know biblical doctrine. They know doctrine well enough so that they are effective in corrupting biblical truth (1 Timothy 4:1-3).

- Demons know about salvation and thus want to keep people from trusting Christ (1 John 4:1-4). They also know that God will one day judge them (Matthew 8:29).

What can demons do?

The Bible also tells us some of the things demons can do. For example, they can possess unusual strength. The demon in one man was so strong that the man was uncontrollable (Mark 5:1-5). In the book of Acts (19:13-16) we read about a demon-possessed man who overpowered seven sons of a Jewish chief priest.

Demons can also cause people to turn to idol worship (Deuteronomy 32:17) and to offer sacrifices to demons (Psalm 106:37). When the spirit of the Lord departed from Saul, a demon terrorized him (1 Samuel 16:14).

During the ministry of Jesus, demons were very active. They caused dumbness (Matthew 9:33), blindness (Matthew 12:22), epilepsy (Matthew 17:15-18), and mental problems (Mark 5:1-20). Demons can also torment people and make them sick (Acts 5:16).

In the last days, the power of demons will be especially evident. For example, during the Tribulation a horde of demons will kill a third of mankind (Revelation 9:13-19), and demons will also perform miraculous signs (Revelation 16:14).

DEMON POSSESSION

SATAN AND HIS DEMONS have influence over our world, but how much of an influence do they have? Can Christians be demon possessed? Some Christians say no, they cannot, while others say believers can be demonized.

Many cultures, both ancient and modern, have believed and continue to believe in demons and demon possession. What does the Bible say about the possibility of demonic influence and possession?

What is the nature of demon possession?

When the New Testament talks about demon possession, it often states that a person "has a demon." For example, Mark 3:30 says, "He has an unclean spirit." Luke 7:33 says, "He has a demon!" And in John 7:20, a crowd told Jesus, "You have a demon!"

In the Gospels the verb *daimonizomai* is used 13 times. This is best translated "to be demon possessed." Alex Konya defined demon possession as "the invasion of a victim's body by a demon (or demons), in which the demon exercises living and sovereign control over the victim, which the victim cannot successfully resist."[7]

A significant number of Christians have suggested that a better word is *demonized* or *demonization*. These individuals suggest this term to imply that a believer might be influenced by rather than possessed by a demon. Fred Dickason, for example, states that there may be "varying degrees" of demonization.[8] We will discuss this more extensively in a moment.

It is also important to note that, in Scripture, the phrase "unclean spirit" is just another way of saying that a person is demon possessed. A man from Gerasenes met Jesus and was described as having an "unclean spirit" (Mark 5:2), and then later he was described as being "demon-possessed" (Mark 5:15-18).

Most Christian authors make a distinction between demon possession and demonic influence. The influence of demons is part of the daily spiritual warfare that all Christians encounter. It is both constant and continuous.

Demon possession, however, is much more than demonic influence. The word *possession* conveys the idea of a demon indwelling a person and controlling his thoughts, emotions, and actions. Merrill Unger makes this distinction between demonic influence and demon possession:

> In demon influence, evil spirits exert power over a person short of actual possession. Such influence may vary from mild harassment to extreme subjection when body and mind become dominated and held in slavery in spirit agents. Christians, as well as non-Christians, can be so influenced. They may be oppressed, vexed, depressed, hindered, and bound by demons.[9]

Demonic influence may affect a person's physical or mental health as well as his spiritual well-being. Demonic possession is a more intrusive form of demonic activity and leads to extremes of involuntary behavior and can even lead to illness.

Each case of demon possession described in the New Testament shows us how tormented the victims were. The two demon-possessed men who met Jesus in the Gadarenes were described as "extremely violent" (Matthew 8:28). A boy brought to Jesus by his father (Mark 9:17) was "mute" because he was "possessed with a spirit." Many of the demon-possessed individuals suffered at the hands of demons (Mark 15:22) and would hurt themselves (Mark 5:5; 9:18-20).

How do people become demon possessed?

The Bible doesn't provide an exhaustive list of the various ways people become demon possessed. It does provide some warnings against certain occultic activities, though the Bible doesn't necessarily say engaging in such practices leads to demon possession. When we hear the stories of evil dictators, mass murderers, and serial killers, we often hear of occultic activities in their background.

In the book of Acts, we find two examples of possible links between demon possession and the occult. In Acts 16:16 a girl is described as having a spirit of divination, which she used to foretell the future. It appears that a demon within her was giving her this information. And the Bible warns us to avoid divination and other forms of the occult: "There shall not be found among you…one who uses divination, one who practices witchcraft, or one who interprets omens, or a sorcerer, or one who casts a spell, or a medium, or a spiritist, or one who calls up the dead" (Deuteronomy 18:10-11).

The other example is in Acts 19, where we read of the city of Ephesus, which was known as a place for occult activities. In the city Paul performed miracles and exorcisms (Acts 19:11-16), which suggests a connection between the occult activities and the number of people who were demon possessed. Those who were released from demonic possession chose to burn their occult literature (verse 19). Even today, Christians who were once involved in the occult report that they encountered demons, spirit guides, and other similar entities.[10]

It also appears that idolatry and demon possession are related as well. In the Old Testament we read of people who were sacrificing to demons (Deuteronomy 32:17; Psalm 106:36-37). In the New Testament Paul wrote, "I say that the things which the Gentiles sacrifice, they sacrifice to demons and not to God; and I do not want you to become sharers in demons. You cannot drink the cup of the Lord and the cup of demons; you cannot partake of the table of the Lord and the table of demons" (1 Corinthians 10:20-21).

Can Christians be demon possessed?

Christian writers are divided on this question. Most say that believers cannot be demon possessed, arguing that God and evil cannot coexist in the same body. They say that because the Holy Spirit indwells a believer, there is no place for a demonic spirit to dwell in that same person.

Some argue that both believers and nonbelievers can be demon possessed. They often point to a few passages in the New Testament that seem to imply that believers in the early church were demon possessed. Let's look at these passages more closely.

1. *Luke 13:11-16*—Here, Jesus healed a woman who was ill and had been bound by Satan "for eighteen long years" (verse 16). The passage also says she was a "daughter of Abraham" (verse 16). Consider these two points: First, we are not told that she was a believer. That she was a daughter of Abraham means she was Jewish, but we are not told if she was a convert to Christianity. Second, the passage does not say she was demon possessed. It only says she was "bound" by Satan. This *could* mean she was demon possessed, but that is not what the passage states.

2. *Acts 5:3*—Acts 5 opens with the story of Ananias and

Sapphira, who sold some land and gave a portion of the money to the apostles, but pretended that they were giving the whole amount. Peter confronted Ananias by asking, "Why has Satan filled your heart to lie to the Holy Spirit, and to keep back some of the price of the land?" The passage does not say that they were demon possessed; only that Satan filled their hearts. The Greek word for "filled" is the same word used in Ephesians 5:18 to talk about the filling of the Holy Spirit. Because the *filling* of the Holy Spirit is different from the *indwelling* of the Holy Spirit, the fact Satan filled their hearts does not necessarily mean they were demon possessed.

What is demonization?

Most often the demonic aspect of spiritual warfare is viewed in terms of either demonic influence or demon possession. Most Christians argue that believers can be influenced or oppressed, but not possessed. Nonbelievers, however, can be both oppressed and possessed. This has been the standard orthodox position presented by most Christian authors.

But a growing number of Christian authors (including Fred Dickason, Mark Bubeck, and Karl Payne) have proposed a third option called *demonization.* Their arguments rest more on experience than on Scripture. They say that the testimonies of thousands of Christians demonstrate that the oppression/possession paradigm does not fit their experience. These thousands say that even though they abide by biblical principles and apply the spiritual disciplines to their lives, they are still tormented by feelings of fear, failure, and condemnation.

The argument for the oppression/demonization/possession paradigm is three-fold. First, the view doesn't violate Scripture. Proponents even say that "it does a better job of incorporating the totality of Scripture on the subject."[11]

Second, it provides an explanation for the spiritual warfare that Christians face on a regular basis and it allows for confrontation and resolution. Third, it passes a reality test. Christians who have been set free from the problems associated with spiritual warfare have learned how to defend themselves from demonic activity.

Proponents also argue that the traditional oppression/possession paradigm does not adequately explain all the trials and temptations Christians face in their lives. Christian missionaries in other countries often talk about witnessing demonic attacks on genuine believers—attacks that go far beyond influence or oppression.

A key verse for these proponents is Ephesians 4:26-27, which says we should not let the sun go down on our anger or we might give Satan "an opportunity" or a "foothold" (NIV). The original Greek word here can refer to an inhabited place or space. Renting out a room to someone does not make that person the owner of the house or apartment. Likewise, it might be possible that demons could get a foothold in our life even though God is still our legal owner (Galatians 2:20).

Critics of this view argue that the body of a believer is the temple of the Holy Spirit (1 Corinthians 6:19). Because all Christians are indwelt by the Holy Spirit (Romans 8:9-11), they believe it is unlikely that a demon could take up residence within a believer. God would never share space with demons or anything evil. In fact, God has "rescued us from the domain of darkness, and transferred us to the kingdom of His beloved Son" (Colossians 1:13). And 1 John 4:4 reminds us, "Greater is He who is in you than he who is in the world."

How should believers respond to this debate?

The various views regarding demons and Christians is an area where Bible-believing teachers disagree, and it is not within the scope of this book to resolve all the questions and criticisms raised by the different views. But here are some important points of application for all believers:

First, because the Bible does not clearly state whether Christians can be demon possessed, it is wise not to be dogmatic about it. Moreover, though the Bible is silent or at least ambiguous about whether Christians can be demon possessed, it definitely does not address how to deal with Christians who might be demon possessed. The fact the Bible is silent or ambiguous on this point seems to indicate it must not be a crucial issue in the Christian life. After all, the Bible tells us that "His divine power has granted to us everything pertaining to life and godliness, through the true knowledge of Him who called us by His own glory and excellence" (2 Peter 1:3). The Bible gives us knowledge of everything pertaining to life and godliness, but it says little or nothing about the matter of demon possession.

Second, the Bible teaches that when it comes to Satan and his demons, we are to be on the defensive, not the offensive. On a number of occasions Scripture tells us to *resist* the devil (Ephesians 6:13; James 4:7; 1 Peter 5:9), and that is a defensive posture. Some translations talk about our need to *stand against* Satan, but even that is a defensive posture. So we who are believers are to resist or stand against Satan, but we are not commanded to go Satan-hunting. We are not to be like those teachers who taunt Satan and "revile angelic majesties" (2 Peter 2:10).

Thomas Ice and Robert Dean explain that a Christian is like a guard who should remain at his post and not go out to engage the enemy:

> Just as a guard who spotted the enemy and went out to engage him would be dangerously exposed to the attacks of the enemy, so a believer is vulnerable to increased satanic attack when he stops resisting and starts attacking.

> Perhaps the reason some churches have so many people who have problems with demons is because they are involved in an aggressive campaign against Satan which has put them in a position of biblical disobedience and opened them up to demonic oppression. We must recognize that the battle is the Lord's and not ours.[12]

We should not go out looking for Satan and his demons. Rather, we are commanded to resist him when he attacks or tempts us.

Can demonic activity be linked to ancestral involvement in the occult?

A number of teachers on spiritual warfare suggest that the sins of our ancestors can provide an opening for demonic involvement in our lives. The assumption is that the sins of one generation are passed on to the next generation. Proponents of this idea claim that there is scriptural support for this view in Exodus 20:5.

Exodus 20:5 is part of the Ten Commandments. It says, "You shall not worship [idols] or serve them; for I, the LORD your God, am a jealous God, visiting the iniquity of the fathers on the children, on the third and the fourth generations of those who hate Me." Proponents argue that demons can control a person while he is alive, and after the person dies, the demons still exist, so they then look for a relative to inhabit in order to continue their demonic activity. Thus, this suggests that demonization is a generational issue.

But that isn't what Exodus 20:5 teaches. The passage actually shows that God's blessings or judgments on the nation of Israel result from the choice of each generation to either follow God's leading or follow after the sins of their ancestors. If one generation sins, that does not necessarily mean that the next generation is under a generational curse. Each of us possesses a free moral will to choose God or to follow the sinful ways of our parents and grandparents.

The Old Testament, in Ezekiel 18, teaches that God's curse falls on each Israelite because of his or her own sins. Verse 20 says, "The person who sins will die. The son will not bear the punishment for the father's iniquity, nor will the father bear the punishment for the son's iniquity; the righteousness of the righteous will be upon himself, and the wickedness of the wicked will be upon himself." This clearly disputes the concept of a generational curse being passed on from one generation to the next. There is no passage in Scripture that teaches that a demonic curse is passed on generationally, and there *are* passages that specifically contradict such a notion.

In the New Testament we have a number of examples of Jesus casting out demons and a few examples of the apostles doing the same. It is worth noting that there is not one case in which a person was under a demonic curse due to ancestral involvement in the occult. If ancestral bondage were truly a major spiritual problem, one would expect the Bible to directly and clearly address the issue. Yet it is essentially silent about the matter.

Can demons be blamed for all the sins of the flesh?

In chapter 2, we learned the three ways we are affected by spiritual warfare: the world, the flesh, and the devil. And we focused at length on the flesh because it has such a major influence on us.

When we consider the various passages about spiritual warfare in Scripture, it is interesting to observe that most of them have to do with the flesh. In the New Testament epistles, there are ten references to demons, yet there are over 50 references to "the flesh" as a major threat to Christians. We also saw in chapter 5 that the few references to demons were mostly descriptive rather than instructive.

Thus we can conclude that the major area of conflict in spiritual warfare is the flesh—much more so than demonic influence. I would think most of us would conclude this from our own personal experience as well.

A person who is living in the flesh is focused on the world and his or her fleshly needs rather than on God and things of the Spirit:

> Those who are according to the flesh set their minds on the things of the flesh, but those who are according to the Spirit, the things of the Spirit. For the mind set on the flesh is death, but the mind set on the Spirit is life and peace, because the mind set on the flesh is hostile toward God; for it does not subject itself to the law of God, for it is not even able to do so, and those who are in the flesh cannot please God (Romans 8:5-8).

We also discovered that even when Satan attempts to attack us, he will use the temptations that affect our flesh in order to achieve his purpose:

> You were dead in your trespasses and sins, in which you formerly walked according to the course of this world, according to the prince of the power of the air, of the spirit that is now working in the sons of disobedience. Among them we too all formerly lived in the lusts of our flesh, indulging the desires of the flesh and of the mind, and were by nature children of wrath, even as the rest (Ephesians 2:1-3).

Therefore, wise and discerning Christians will guard themselves against the impact the flesh can have on their spiritual life.

A believer must not allow Satan to get a foothold (Ephesians 4:26-27).

The apostle Paul exhorts us to not live in the flesh, but rather, to live by the Spirit:

> You are not in the flesh but in the Spirit, if indeed the Spirit of God dwells in you. But if anyone does not have the Spirit of Christ, he does not belong to Him. If Christ is in you, though the body is dead because of sin, yet the spirit is alive because of righteousness. But if the Spirit of Him who raised Jesus from the dead dwells in you, He who raised Christ Jesus from the dead will also give life to your mortal bodies through His Spirit who dwells in you. So then, brethren, we are under obligation, not to the flesh, to live according to the flesh—for if you are living according to the flesh, you must die; but if by the Spirit you are putting to death the deeds of the body, you will live (Romans 8:9-13).

Even in his day, the world-renowned evangelist D.L. Moody (1837–1899) was concerned that believers were paying more attention to Satan and demons than they were to the influence of their own flesh. He said, "Someone has said there is always a devil at our right hand: though if we resist the devil he will flee from us. But it is different with the flesh; the flesh cleaves to us. I believe that the flesh is the worst enemy we have."[13]

Some spiritual warfare teachers go so far as to say that there are actually demons with names based on many of these temptations. They say that these demons have names such as *Lust* or *Envy* or *Murder*. Therefore they teach that we should cast out the demon of lust in order to be free of lust, or that we should cast out the demon of envy in order to rid ourselves of feelings of envy.

That is not what the Bible teaches. Galatians 5:19-21, for

example, teaches that these temptations are "the deeds of the flesh." James 1:14 teaches that we are tempted and "carried away" by our own lust. So not everything related to temptation and sin can be blamed on demons. Much of it is actually the result of the flesh's influence.

7

ANGELS

THERE ARE MANY POPULAR NOTIONS about angels (both good and fallen) that are confused and often incorrect. Most religions have a belief in angels, so some of the confusion comes from the various views these religions have. One example of an incorrect notion is the thought that angels are former human beings who, after dying, came to inhabit a glorified body. But Jesus taught that angels are different from humans. For example, they do not marry or reproduce like humans (Matthew 22:30). Angels are not glorified human beings.

There are also modern skeptics who believe that angels don't exist. And there are others who believe that a reference to angels is merely a figure of speech to imply God's power working on earth. But we don't have to speculate about whether angels are figurative or don't exist because the Bible clearly affirms their existence. They are mentioned at least 108 times in the Old Testament and 165 times in the New Testament. The word "angel" comes from the Greek word *angelos,* which means "messenger." The corresponding Hebrew word also means "messenger." Angels are God's messengers to earth.

Were angels created by God?

The Bible clearly teaches that angels have not always existed (Nehemiah 9:6; Psalm 148:2-5). That is, God created them. But the Bible does not tell us when that occurred.

The Bible teaches that God is the creator of all things, and that would surely include angels. Colossians 1:16-17 says, "By Him all things were created, both in the heavens and on earth, visible and invisible, whether thrones or dominions or rulers or authorities—all things have been created through Him and for Him. He is before all things, and in Him all things hold together." John 1:3 says that "all things came into being through Him, and apart from Him nothing came into being." It would seem that angels must be included in this statement about "all things" coming into being.

Some speculate that the creation of the angels occurred during the creation of the heavens (Genesis 1:1). While that seems logical, the Bible does not give us that information. But it is reasonable to assume that they were created by that time, for Job 38:7 says "the sons of God shouted for joy" when God laid the foundations of the earth. It appears that the angels rejoiced when the creation was complete.

How many angels are there?

The Bible does not reveal the number of angels in existence, but various passages suggest there could be millions of them. The writer of Hebrews speaks of "an innumerable company of angels" (Hebrews 12:22 KJV).

David describes thousands of angels in the sky and stars: "The chariots of God are myriads, thousands upon thousands" (Psalm 68:17). Ten thousand angels came down on Mount Sinai to confirm the presence of God as he gave the Ten Commandments to Moses (Deuteronomy 33:2). The book of Revelation talks about "ten thousand times ten thousand" angels ministering to the Lamb of God (Revelation 5:11 KJV).

Can we see angels?

Angels are "ministering spirits" (Hebrews 1:14), or spirit beings, so they are invisible to human beings. But angels do occasionally take on a physical form. Some theologians have suggested that it is probably good that we don't see angels, for we would probably be tempted to worship them. We see in the Bible that often when angels appear, human beings react as if they are in the presence of God.

We are not to worship angels (Colossians 2:18); God alone is worthy of our worship. We should not worship the creation, but rather, we should worship the Creator (Romans 1:24-25). And Jesus Christ is the Creator of all things and thus is worthy of our worship.

When angels appear in their heavenly form (not disguised as humans), they have a blinding brilliance of light that surrounds them. The angel who rolled away the stone from the tomb of Jesus was dressed in white and shone with a dazzling brilliance (Matthew 28:3).

Daniel saw an angel and described him in this way: "His body also was like beryl, his face had the appearance of lightning, his eyes were like flaming torches, his arms and feet like the gleam of polished bronze, and the sound of his words like the sound of a tumult" (Daniel 10:6). The apostle John saw an angel and said that a "rainbow was upon his head" and that "his face was like the sun" (Revelation 10:1).

Do angels have wings?

Almost every picture you ever see of angels depicts them as

creatures that look remarkably human except for the fact that they have wings on their backs. There are two problems with that depiction. First, angels are not humans. It's true the Bible reports that angels can sometimes appear as humans. But it is likely that their true form probably does not resemble that of human beings.

Second, the Bible confirms that some types of angels have wings: seraphim and cherubim. The angels whom Isaiah saw in his vision had wings (Isaiah 6:2). The seraphim in that passage had three pairs of wings: one pair covered their face, one pair covered their feet, and the third pair was used for flying. The cherubim (Exodus 25; Ezekiel 10) had four wings each (Ezekiel 1:11). While the cherubim and seraphim represent two of the highest orders of angels, this does not mean that all angels have wings.

It is important to remember that angels are spirit beings (Hebrews 1:14) and thus probably do not need wings to fly. Spirit beings do not need the help of wind resistance to fly because they reside outside the physical laws of the universe.

The Bible does report that angels fly. In addition to the statement in Isaiah 6:2 that says the seraphim "flew," we have the description by the apostle John of an "angel flying in midheaven" (Revelation 14:6). The angel Gabriel was able to "fly swiftly" (Daniel 9:21 ASV) when he came to Daniel.

So we can conclude that some angels have wings, but cannot definitively say that all of them do. And, they do not need wings to fly and swiftly carry out God's commands.

What are some of the tasks of angels?

The Bible describes many tasks and activities of angels. And it tells us they are powerful creatures. Paul refers to them as God's "mighty angels" (2 Thessalonians 1:7). They are certainly up to the tasks they are given, though their primary activity seems to be praising God.

Here are some of the activities reported of angels:

Worshipping and praising God—This appears to be one of the primary activities of angels. We see this in the description of the seraphim who worship God (Isaiah 6:1-7). We also see this in the last book of the Bible (Revelation 4–5).

Answering prayer—Angels were sometimes used as a means of answering the prayers of God's people (Daniel 9:20-24; 10:10-12; Acts 12:1-17).

Declaring—Angels are messengers who come to earth to communicate God's will and word to humans. Angels helped reveal the law to Moses (Acts 7:52-53) and to Daniel. We see in the book of the Revelation that they will also do this in the future.

Guiding—Angels also guide humans in particular tasks. An angel gave specific instructions to Joseph about the birth of Jesus (Matthew 1–2). Angels appeared to the women at the tomb (Luke 24:1-8), to Philip (Acts 8:26), and to Cornelius (Acts 10:1-8).

Protecting—Angels protected Shadrach, Meshach, and Abednego in the fiery furnace (Daniel 3). An angel also protected Daniel in the lions' den (Daniel 6).

Delivering—Angels have been used to get God's people out of danger (Acts 5; 12).

Providing—Angels have provided food to those in need. This was done for Elijah (1 Kings 19:5-6) and Jesus (Matthew 4:11).

Encouraging—Angels encouraged the apostles to keep preaching after helping to release them from prison (Acts 5:19-20) and revealed to Paul that everyone on a ship taking him to Rome would survive an impending shipwreck (Acts 27:23-25).

How are angels organized?

The Bible suggests there are different ranks of angels. While it does not reveal any kind of organizational chart, there are some passages that help us to infer certain aspects of their authority, organization, and responsibility.

Archangel

The Bible calls Michael "the archangel" (Jude 9). The title *arch* implies that he is the head angel. There is also reason to believe that Satan was an archangel before he rebelled against God.

In the Old Testament, Michael is identified with the nation of Israel. For example, in the book of Daniel he is called "Michael your prince" (10:21). Two chapters later he is called "Michael, the great prince who stands guard over the sons of your people" (12:1).

In the New Testament, Michael is the archangel who leads the armies of angels against Satan and his demons (Revelation 12:7-12). This battle at the end of the age will be the greatest example of good versus evil and will be fought on Earth and in the heavenly places.

Gabriel

Only two angels are mentioned by name in the Bible: Michael and Gabriel. Gabriel may not be an archangel (although some Christian traditions view him as an archangel), but in Scripture, he is also given great prominence. He is often referred to as God's messenger because he appears four times bearing good news (Daniel 8:16; 9:21; Luke 1:19,26). While it is true that he brings God's message, it is questionable as to whether he blows a trumpet when he delivers this news.

Seraphim

In Isaiah 6:1 we read about seraphim who are praising God. They are positioned above the throne of God, and they can help purify people such as Isaiah (6:7). They have two wings that cover their face, two wings that cover their feet, and two wings for flying.

Cherubim

The cherubim apparently have wings and hands, but are also described as being "full of eyes" and having "whirling wheels" (Ezekiel 10:12-13). They are found standing on the right side of the temple and were incorporated into the design of the Ark of the Covenant (Exodus 25). They are constantly glorifying God and we find them mentioned often in the Old Testament (see Psalm 80:1; 99:1).

How powerful are angels?

Apparently angels are very powerful creatures, but they are not all-powerful like God, who is omnipotent. Paul refers to them as "mighty angels" (2 Thessalonians 1:7). The Greek word translated "mighty" is the same word from which we get the English word *dynamite.* Apparently their power is like dynamite.

Peter talks about "angels who are greater in might and power" than human beings (2 Peter 2:11). So they have might and power and can execute God's commands and judgments on the earth. In Daniel we see that one angel "shut the mouths of the lions" to protect him (6:22).

God also executes His judgment through angels. "He sent upon them his burning anger, fury and indignation and trouble, a band of destroying angels" (Psalm 78:49). And God commands His angels to guard the righteous (Psalm 91:11). David talked about how God's angels are "mighty in strength" (Psalm 103:20).

We also see the power of angels in Bible passages about the last days. Angels will be used to gather "those who commit lawlessness, and will throw them into the furnace of fire" (Matthew 13:41). Jesus taught that angels will be responsible for the separation of the righteous from the wicked (Matthew 13:49-50). He also said that when He returns, He will come with angels (Matthew 16:27). And the angels will gather the righteous at the time of the rapture (Matthew 24:31).

Angels will also execute judgment against Satan in the last days. "Then I saw an angel coming down from heaven, holding the key of the abyss and a great chain in his hand. And he laid hold of the dragon, the serpent of old, who is the devil and Satan, and bound him for a thousand years" (Revelation 20:1-2).

Does each person have a guardian angel?

Given the fascination people have with angels, it is not surprising that many believe that each person has a guardian angel. This idea has also been promoted within the church. Some of the early Christian writers affirmed their belief in guardian angels along with theologians such as Origen and Thomas Aquinas.

Some Christians teach that guardian angels surround us, protect us, and intercede for us. This belief is based upon a couple Bible passages.

In Exodus 23:20 God told the people of Israel, "Behold, I am going to send an angel before you to guard you along the way and to bring you into the place which I have prepared." And in Psalm 91:11 we read, "He will give His angels charge concerning you, to guard you in all your ways." While these passages do talk about angels as guards, neither specifically says each of us has a guardian angel. The first passage dealt with God's provision for the Israelites as they engaged in the conquest of the Promised Land. The second mentions angels as guards, but it doesn't specifically say that each person has a guardian angel.

In the Old Testament, we see that the archangel Michael was

assigned to the nation of Israel (Daniel 10:21; 12:1). But we do not see any place in the Bible where an angel is assigned to an individual person. Sometimes angels were *sent* to a person, but they weren't assigned as a guardian of that person.

It is also important to note that nowhere in the Bible do we see the word *guardian*. This doesn't mean guardian angels don't exist. It simply means that there are no passages that refer to guardian angels.

Among the New Testament passages said to suggest guardian angels exist is Matthew 18:10, which says, "See that you do not despise one of these little ones, for I say to you that their angels in heaven continually see the face of My Father who is in heaven." It is possible that the "little ones" could apply either to people who believe in God (verse 6) or to little children (verses 3-5). It is possible that this passage is teaching that angels perform a ministry on behalf of God's children; it is possible it is teaching that each person has a guardian angel.

Another passage is Hebrews 1:14, which provides insight into the function of angels: "Are they not all ministering spirits, sent out to render service for the sake of those who will inherit salvation?" Holy angels minister and render service to believers. They also protect (2 Kings 6:13-17; Daniel 6:20-23), guide (Matthew 1:20-21; Acts 8:26), and make provision (Genesis 21; 1 Kings 19:5-7). While they provide all these services for God's people, we don't see any indication they are assigned to one individual throughout his or her life.

A significant problem with the concept of guardian angels is that the idea can distract us from God and His ministry in our lives. For a person to concentrate on guardian angels can make that person take his eyes off God. For some, the supposed guardian angel could even replace God. Some might even pray to an angel instead of God.

God is to be worshipped, not angels (Exodus 20:1-6; Colossians 2:18). Prayer, adoration, and worship are reserved for God alone. There are some people who promote angels and also acknowledge God, yet they rarely mention the Son of God. John 5:23 reminds us that "He who does not honor the Son does not honor the Father who sent Him."

Also, a fixation on angels is not only biblically incorrect, it is dangerous. As we have already learned, not all angels are good. Second Corinthians 11:14 reminds us that "Satan disguises himself as an angel of light." Satan and his fellow fallen angels can deceive us, so we would be wise not to attempt to contact angels much less pray to them.

The Bible warns us to stay away from any communication with the spirit world. Deuteronomy 18:10-11 says, "There shall not be found among you anyone who makes his son or his daughter pass through the fire, one who uses divination, one who practices witchcraft, or one who interprets omens, or a sorcerer, or one who casts a spell, or a medium, or a spiritist, or one who calls up the dead." Leviticus 19:31 says, "Do not turn to mediums or spiritists; do not seek them out to be defiled by them. I am the LORD your God."

8

UNBIBLICAL MISCONCEPTIONS

WHEN IT COMES TO THE SUBJECTS of angels, demons, and spiritual warfare, there are many unbiblical misconceptions people hold to. The current angelmania encourages us to contact angels and attract them to us. Television programs and movies promote false views of both good and fallen angels. Popular books and other literature teach unbiblical views of spiritual beings. What are those misconceptions, and how can we respond to them?

Is Jesus an angel?

There are some who say that Jesus was just an angel. This confusion arises from two sources: theological error and artistic interpretation. In the second century, a heretical group known as the Gnostics taught that Jesus did not have a real body but was only a spirit who appeared to have a human form. In other words, Jesus was like an angel. This view was rejected and even condemned by the Christians in the first few centuries of the church.

And today, there are some who teach that Jesus was an angel. For example, Jehovah's Witnesses say that Jesus was Michael the

Archangel. The name *Michael* means "who is like God." So they argue that Jesus is not Jehovah, but an angel.

The artistic renderings of Jesus in many famous paintings may have encouraged some to believe that Jesus was an angel. Some artists have indicated angels in their paintings by placing a halo above their heads. And some of them also painted Jesus with a halo to show His divine nature. Over time, this depiction of Jesus came to give the impression that Jesus was an angel (perhaps king of the angels).

Jesus was not and is not an angel. In fact, the Bible describes Jesus as the Creator (John 1:1-3; Colossians 1:16-17), which means He created the angels. What's more, God the Father called Jesus God (Hebrews 1:8). After the resurrection, the apostles declared Jesus to be God (John 20:28, Philippians 2:6; Colossians 2:9; Titus 2:13). And we are told that the name of Jesus is above all other names (Philippians 2:9). Jesus is not an angel; He is God.

Do people become angels when they arrive in heaven?

Often during a funeral someone will say that the recently departed is now an angel in heaven. And because a funeral is the last place anyone would want to split theological hairs, the comment often goes unchallenged. But is it true that people become angels when they get to heaven?

It is understandable that people would assume this because there are some similarities between humans and angels. In fact, Paul tells us that we will one day receive "heavenly bodies" (1 Corinthians 15:40) and that our earthy tent will be replaced by "a building from God" (2 Corinthians 5:1). So in that limited sense, we will be like the angels.

Jesus also taught that one day we will be "like angels in heaven" (Matthew 22:30) in the sense that we will no longer marry. But notice that Jesus says we will be *like* angels, not that we will *become* angels. What's more, there are significant differences between human beings and angels.

Here are a couple of the differences: First, God made humans a little lower than the angels (Psalm 8:5; Hebrews 2:7), and in our present state, every one of us is born, will age, and die. By contrast, angels were created in their present state and do not age or die. Second, human beings can experience salvation by God's grace (Ephesians 2:8-9), but angels cannot. Humans are born with a sin nature, and if we place our trust in Jesus Christ, we will someday have a glorified body (Philippians 3:21). By contrast, angels are not born with a sin nature. And those angels who have fallen cannot experience salvation, and are destined to eternal condemnation. They have no chance at redemption, as humans do.

Should we pray to angels?

Throughout the centuries there have been various religious groups and leaders who have prayed to angels and encouraged others to do the same. But is this practice biblical?

First, we should remember what Jesus instructed us to do when we pray. We are to pray to the Father in Jesus' name. In John 14:13-14, Jesus said, "I will do whatever you ask in my name, so that the Son may bring glory to the Father. You may ask me for anything in my name, and I will do it" (NIV).

We can also pray with confidence: "This is the confidence we have in approaching God: that if we ask anything according to his will, he hears us. And if we know that he hears us—whatever we ask—we know that we have what we asked of him" (1 John 5:14-15 NIV). Notice that we are to pray to God and not to any other being. Angels are created beings and thus are not on the same level as God (and the persons of the Godhead).

Also, we are specifically commanded not to worship angels:

"Let no one keep defrauding you of your prize by delighting in self-abasement and the worship of the angels, taking his stand on visions he has seen inflated without cause by his fleshly mind" (Colossians 2:18-19). Here the apostle Paul warned believers about false teachers who claimed to have special revelation and supernatural insights because of their worship of angels.

In the Bible, whenever someone was tempted to worship angels, he was commanded to stop. For example, we find two places in the book of Revelation where the apostle John was so overwhelmed by angelic creatures who appeared to him that he bowed down to worship them.

- Revelation 19:10—"I fell at his feet to worship him. But he said to me, 'Do not do that; I am a fellow servant of yours and your brethren who hold the testimony of Jesus; worship God. For the testimony of Jesus is the spirit of prophecy.'"

- Revelation 22:8-9—"I, John, am the one who heard and saw these things. And when I heard and saw, I fell down to worship at the feet of the angel who showed me these things. But he said to me, 'Do not do that. I am a fellow servant of yours and of your brethren the prophets and of those who heed the words of this book. Worship God.'"

Those who encourage us to pray to angels argue that such prayer is not worship. While that may be true, it would be easy to begin to worship a creature to whom you direct your prayers. Yet angels are creatures and servants of God and do not deserve worship.

Worshipping angels is dangerous because, as we have previously noted, some angels are not holy but demonic. Paul warns that "Satan disguises himself as an angel of light" (2 Corinthians 11:14) and his followers portray themselves as messengers of righteousness (2 Corinthians 11:15). When we pray to an angel, we may think we are praying to a holy angel when we are actually praying to a demonic angel.

While it's true that we should not pray to angels, we do find that God uses angels to answer our prayers. In Scripture, we can find examples of God using angels to answer the prayers of believers (Daniel 9:20-24; 10:10-12; Acts 12:1-17).

Do angels provide new revelation today?

We live in a society in which many religious teachers talk about angels and spirit guides. Angels are said to guide us spiritually and give us additional revelation. But the apostle Paul warned that even if "an angel from heaven should preach to you a gospel contrary to what we have preached to you, he is to be accursed" (Galatians 1:8).

Yes, angels have been involved in communicating God's revelation in the past, but they did so at God's direction. They were *God's* messengers (both the Hebrew and Greek words translated "angel" mean "messenger"). A number of New Testament passages tell us that God used angels to reveal His Word (Acts 7:53; Galatians 3:19; Hebrews 2:2).

But the Bible also warns us to beware of anyone claiming to bring new revelation. This applies to anyone who says he or she received a new revelation from an angel. That's because Satan and his demons are deceivers who promote false doctrine (2 Corinthians 11:1-13; 1 Timothy 4:1).

The current "angelmania" in our society today provides ample opportunity for spiritual deception. Books and seminar leaders talk about how to contact angels and how to attract them into your life. They describe attempts by the angels to pass on additional revelations from God, or supposedly hidden knowledge that will now be revealed in these last days.

By contrast, the Bible says we have everything we need for life and godliness (2 Peter 1:3). Thus hidden and esoteric knowledge actually comes from fallen angels who are attempting to pervert true, biblical doctrine and promote false doctrine. God's angels are supposed to be messengers, not teachers.

Can Christians bind Satan?

The Bible tells us to put on the whole armor of God so that we can stand against Satan (Ephesians 6:11-16). It also tells us to resist Satan (James 4:7) so that he will flee from us. And it even admonishes us not to give a place for the devil to work in our lives (Ephesians 4:27). But does the Bible say that we can *bind* Satan?

There are a few passages that some spiritual warfare teachers use to argue that Christians can bind Satan. One is Matthew 12:29: "How can anyone enter the strong man's house and carry off his property, unless he first binds the strong man? And then he will plunder his house." The context of this passage is important. Jesus was responding to the Pharisees, who accused Him of casting out demons by the power of Beelzebul, the ruler of the demons.

Jesus' point was this: He had to be *stronger* than Satan because He was able to cast out Satan's demons. In other words, He was able to go into the strong man's house (Satan's domain) and win the spiritual battle. But there is nothing in this passage that teaches the *believers* can bind Satan. Some commentators believe that Jesus may have been foreshadowing the fact that Satan would be bound in the future during the thousand years known as the Millennium (Revelation 20:1-3).

Two other passages often used to teach that Christians can bind Satan are Matthew 16:19 and 18:18. In the first, Jesus tells

Peter, "Whatever you bind on earth shall have been bound in heaven, and whatever you loose on earth shall have been loosed in heaven" (Matthew 16:19). Jesus then says essentially the same thing to the other disciples in Matthew 18:18.

In both passages, the focus is on the fact that Jesus' disciples will have authority to tell people on earth what God has already declared in heaven. The words "bind" and "loose" were commonly used in that day to mean "forbid" and "allow." You could translate the words as "unlawful" and "lawful." Essentially Jesus was giving the disciples the authority to declare what was on God's mind in heaven. They had authority, as future apostles, to prohibit and permit the laws and actions that would be part of the New Testament church. We see examples of this in the book of Acts (for example, Acts 15). Jesus was not giving them the ability to bind Satan or demons.

Did the devil make me do it?

Whenever a horrible crime takes place (a mother drowns her children, or a killer stalks a university campus), some people are quick to explain the behavior by saying that the devil made him or her do it. But is it always true that when an evil act takes place Satan is behind that person's actions?

The question brings to mind the words of comedian Flip Wilson. On his television show, he would dress up as his alter ego Geraldine and exclaim, "The devil made me do it!" Quickly the catchphrase caught on and became a part of everyday conversation. But it isn't good theology.

Some psychotic killers may hear voices in their head and believe that the devil made them carry out their actions. And while it is possible that Satan did indeed "order" their heinous acts, it is also possible that the human sin nature, possibly encumbered by mental imbalance, is the source of the problem.

As we learned earlier, Satan and his demons try to make us fall into sin all the time. We are instructed to be on our guard and make sure "that Satan will not tempt [us]" (1 Corinthians 7:5). James tells us to "Resist the devil and he will flee from you. Draw near to God and He will draw near to you" (James 4:7-8).

Believers are given the power to resist evil, but they are nevertheless tempted to do sinful acts. Likewise, nonbelievers are tempted but most likely have less ability to resist those temptations. And so in a general sense, the devil did make them do it, but they still had some ability to resist the temptation toward evil.

As we have already noted, demon possession is a real possibility and may indeed explain some of the horrible acts people have done through the ages. But we should never discount the reality that human beings are flawed (Romans 3:23) and live in a fallen world (Genesis 3).

The Bible teaches us that God does not tempt us to sin (James 1:13). But it also teaches, in the next verse, that we can be tempted and "carried away and enticed" by our own lust (James 1:14). While it is true that Satan tempts us, we should never discount the fact that our own flesh entices us, too. And whoever or whatever tempts us, we have the power to choose not to sin.

Can we contact the dead through spirits?

Mediums, channelers, and psychics often talk about making contact with "the other side" through spirits and spirit guides. Many such individuals are on television and have written bestseller books. How should a Christian respond to the claims such people make about contacting the dead?

First, the Bible specifically warns us not to consult with spirits (Leviticus 19:26-31; Isaiah 8:19) or to engage in divination (Deuteronomy 18:9-12). We are not to make contact with the spirit world. A spirit, a spirit guide, or even an angel bringing news of a loved one who is dead is most likely a demon disguised in some way.

Second, the messages from spirit guides are usually contrary to Scripture. Galatians 1:8 says, "Even if we, or an angel from heaven, should preach to you a gospel contrary to what we have preached to you, he is to be accursed!" We are to reject the false teachings and theological errors of spirits and spirit guides.

What about the incident during which King Saul consulted a medium? This took place late in the life of Saul, after he had continually disobeyed God and strayed from the faith. It got to the point that God removed His Holy Spirit from Saul. Before a key battle, Saul cried out to God for guidance but did not receive an answer (1 Samuel 28:6). So he told one of his servants to "seek for me a woman who is a medium, that I may go to her and inquire of her" (1 Samuel 28:7). The irony in this is that Saul had earlier ordered all mediums and spiritists removed from the land. Nevertheless, his servants found one. Saul then disguised himself and visited the medium at Endor, who communicated with the dead.

Saul asked the medium to bring Samuel back from the dead (1 Samuel 28:11). She did so, and was surprised when Samuel appeared. That may have been because up to now, she had faked contact with the dead. She was obviously surprised when Samuel appeared, and she "cried out with a loud voice" (1 Samuel 28:12).

Some have suggested that the medium was a fraud and playing a trick on Saul. But her reaction shows that she was surprised by Samuel's appearance (that wouldn't have been the case if his appearance were merely a trick). Others have suggested that a demon impersonated Samuel and appeared to Saul. But Saul knew Samuel very well and believed he was talking to the spirit of Samuel. Also, the message Samuel brought (1 Samuel 28:16-19) doesn't seem like one that would come from a demon. So it is quite possible that the real spirit of Samuel did in fact appear before Saul and the medium of Endor.

So does Saul's experience indicate that we can contact the dead? Note that this is an isolated example of such in Scripture, and that God never indicates any sign of approval over Saul's actions. We are simply told *what* happened, and we see no evidence we are to do likewise. It seems that God permitted the actual spirit of Samuel to speak, and Samuel announced that Saul and his sons would be killed and that the army of Israel would fall into the hands of the Philistines (1 Samuel 28:19). This is a one-time miraculous event that God allowed in order to bring judgment on Saul for breaking the law by consulting a medium (Deuteronomy 18:9-12).

Clearly, we should not contact the spirit world nor consult with mediums and psychics. Some such individuals may merely be charlatans, but even so, we should stay away from anyone claiming to have the ability to contact the spirit world.

A FINAL WORD

THE THEME RUNNING THROUGHOUT this book is captured in Ephesians 6:12: "Our struggle is not against flesh and blood, but against the rulers, against the powers, against the world forces of this darkness, against the spiritual forces of wickedness in the heavenly places."

And believers have spiritual weapons that can tear down strongholds and philosophies that are in opposition to God:

> Though we walk in the flesh, we do not war according to the flesh, for the weapons of our warfare are not of the flesh, but divinely powerful for the destruction of fortresses. We are destroying speculations and every lofty thing raised up against the knowledge of God, and we are taking every thought captive to the obedience of Christ (2 Corinthians 10:3-5).

These spiritual weapons are available to *every* believer.

But what if you have never placed your trust in Jesus Christ? Then you need to take an important first step in order to be prepared for spiritual warfare. The Bible says, "If you confess with your mouth Jesus as Lord, and believe in your heart that God raised Him from the dead, you will be saved" (Romans 10:9). Your salvation begins with your confession of your sins (Romans 3:23) and a willingness to believe in the resurrection of Jesus Christ (1 Corinthians 15:13-20).

Finally, we should all live by grace: "For by grace you have been saved through faith; and that not of yourselves, it is the gift of God; not as a result of works, so that no one may boast" (Ephesians 2:8-9). We become a child of God by God's grace through faith in Christ. And we are to live each day in God's grace—a grace that is sufficient: "My grace is sufficient for you, for power is perfected in weakness" (2 Corinthians 12:9). Live in God's grace and be ready to persevere through spiritual battle, for "greater is He who is in you than he who is in the world" (1 John 4:4).

BIBLIOGRAPHY

Tony Evans, *The Truth About Spiritual Warfare* (Chicago: Moody, 2000).

Tony Evans, *The Truth About Angels and Demons* (Chicago: Moody, 2005.

Billy Graham, *Angels: God's Secret Agents* (Waco, TX: Word, 1975).

Thomas Ice and Robert Dean, *A Holy Rebellion* (Eugene, OR: Harvest House, 1990).

C.S. Lewis, *The Screwtape Letters* (New York: Macmillan, 1961).

Robert Lightner, *Angels, Satan and Demons* (Nashville, TN: Word, 1998).

Erwin Lutzer, *Seven Snares of the Enemy* (Chicago: Moody, 2001).

Karl Payne, *Spiritual Warfare* (Sammamish, WA: Cross Training Press, 2008).

NOTES

1. Thomas Ice and Robert Dean, *A Holy Rebellion: Strategy for Spiritual Warfare* (Eugene, OR: Harvest House Publishers, 1990), 30.

2. Ibid., 77.

3. Erwin Lutzer, *Seven Snares of the Enemy* (Chicago: Moody Press, 2001).

4. Ibid., 33.

5. Ibid., 118.

6. *Pew Forum on Religion & Public Life,* 2008, http://religions.pewforum.org/–"68 percent of Americans believe angels and demons are active in the world."

7. Alex Konya, *Demons: A Biblically Based Perspective* (Schaumburg, IL: Regular Baptist, 1990), 20-23.

8. Fred Dickason, *Demon Possession and the Christian* (Wheaton, IL: Crossway, 1987), 40.

9. Merrill F. Unger, *Demons in the World Today* (Wheaton, IL: Tyndale, 1971), 113.

10. Marcia Montenegro, *SpellBound: The Paranormal Seduction of Today's Kids* (Colorado Springs: David C. Cook, 2006); Johanna Michelson, *The Beautiful Side of Evil* (Eugene, OR: Harvest House, 1982).

11. Karl Payne, *Devils and Demons* (Redmond, WA: Transferable Cross Training Foundation, 2008), 11; Karl Payne, *Spiritual Warfare* (Sammamish, WA: Cross Training Press, 2008).

12. Ice and Dean, *A Holy Rebellion,* 136.

13. W.H. Daniels, ed. *Moody: His Words, Works, and Workers* (New York: Nelson & Phillips, 1877), 389.

Other Harvest House Books
by Kerby Anderson

HOMOSEXUALITY
A sensitive and factual survey of a difficult topic, this book addresses the essentials you need to know about controversial issues such as the causes of homosexuality, the legalization of same-sex marriages, popular myths about homosexuality, and whether it's possible for homosexuals to change.

INTELLIGENT DESIGN
Voices on both sides of the evolution versus intelligent design debate say that science backs them up. But both cannot be right. This book carefully examines the scientific evidence and digs deep for the facts, using the latest research.

ISLAM
Do Christians and Muslims worship the same God? Is Islam a religion of peace? Does the Qur'an support the martyrdom of suicide bombers? How do the Bible and the Qur'an contradict each other? What is the extent of the threat from radical Islam? These questions and more are answered from a biblical perspective.

HARVEST HOUSE
PUBLISHERS